Christian Studies
Golden Children's Bible

Part I

The Creation
The Patriarchs
The Exodus

Teacher Guide

Christian Studies I
Teacher Manual
By Cheryl Lowe, Leigh Lowe, and Taylor Worley

Published by:

Memoria Press
www.MemoriaPress.com

First Edition 2006
ISBN # 978-1-930953-90-1

Contents

Introduction

The Memoria Press *Christian Studies Series* is a means of educating our children in the most magnificent and meaningful story ever told—the Bible. For this task, both the substance and form have been selected carefully. What is the substance of Christian Studies?

Beyond all other sacred or religious texts, the Bible contains the crucial narrative for all human history. Thus, more than just a great story, it is *the* story! Uniquely more than a mere book, the Bible remains God's personal self-disclosure of His will and ways to the world He created. From the first glorious moments in the Garden of Eden to the arresting visions of Saint John in Revelation, God has been calling out a people to bear His name. In following the story of that rescued people, we find the Salvation History of God, the story of redemption. The ultimate significance of Salvation History, however, is not found merely in the individual stories along the way, but rather in the amazing way the stories link together. In this way, we desire to tell *God's story* through the stories of Abraham, Moses, or David.

Therefore, to preserve the unity of the story, it is fitting that our students should encounter the text of the Bible in the storybook form of *The Golden Children's Bible*. *The Golden Children's Bible* is very close to a simplified Bible. It is not a retelling of Bible stories by a writer with a point of view or a writer whose personality or theology intrudes itself upon the story. The language of *The Golden Children's Bible* is based on the King James Bible, the poetic and literary version of Scripture; it communicates the sacredness of Holy Scripture in a way no other version does. The pictures in *The Golden Children's Bible* are also significant as a teaching tool. This dignified presentation of *The Golden Children's Bible* preserves the reverence we want our students to maintain for the Bible.

However, Memoria Press' *Christian Studies Series* will work well with any other Bible storybook that you may choose or, better yet, with the Bible itself.

With every story, the wonder and awe of the experience depends upon how well the story is told. So, how much more should we strive to engage the hearts and imaginations of our students when we tell the story of God's dealings with mankind? We have made it our goal to avoid trite, simplistic presentations of these magnificent stories. Rather, our task is to communicate effectively both the complexity and breadth of God's Salvation History. How can our students experience a deep sense of awe at the appearance of Jesus Christ, the fulfillment of all of God's promises, unless they feel the Old Testament groans of expectation and longing, such as those found in the period of the Judges or during the Exile? Therefore, we have developed this curriculum for that type of careful narrative approach.

In sum, we believe that our *Christian Studies Series* provides students with a solid foundation of biblical knowledge, which parents can use to enrich young lives in spiritual truths and form them in Christ-like character. Teachers, students, and parents, enjoy the wonder and majesty of God's unfolding story.

Teaching Guidelines

Background Summary

Bible stories have meaning and significance beyond the literal historic events. In order to help you convey the spiritual significance of each story and its place in Salvation History, we have included a section in each lesson of this guide called **Background and Summary**. Please take the time to read this section before you study the lesson. You will be richly rewarded and so will your children.

Read Story

Read *The Golden Children's Bible* selection; pages are at the top left-hand margin of each lesson. If you are using the Bible instead of, or in addition to, *The Golden Children's Bible*, the relevant chapters are at the top right-hand margin. Students should take turns reading aloud in class, with teacher assistance in pronunciation and word meanings. *The Golden Children's Bible*, in and of itself, is a valuable reading curriculum, containing elevated and poetic language, noble and uplifting stories, and advanced vocabulary.

There are THREE activities to reinforce important facts in each lesson, Facts to Know, Comprehension Questions, and Activities.

1. Facts to Know

The Facts to Know section highlights important people, places, events, or terms with concise definitions. Pronounce words for students and have them pronounce after you. Point out entries with unusual spelling. You may want to include some words on weekly spelling tests.

2. Comprehension Questions

It is not necessary to write a complete sentence for every question in the study guide. If time is limited, answer some questions orally or allow one-word answers. However, the process of composing and copying complete sentences, as described below, is a valuable composition lesson, so be sure to include this activity in your weekly lesson.

Call on individual students to read a question and give an answer. When you have enough information from students or from consulting the text, write a complete one- or two-sentence answer on the board for students to copy. For third graders, copying from the board with accuracy can be a challenging exercise. Our teachers use different colored markers for answers and write three to four answers on the board before erasing and beginning over. In addition to reviewing the content of the story and understanding its significance, students learn much from copying answers from the board: spelling, composition, punctuation, accuracy, neatness, and vocabulary.

As students gain skill in answering questions, you can increase the difficulty of this section. First, continue to take oral answers for each question, but instead of composing a complete sentence for students to copy, write key words on the board, and guide students in the difficult art of composing complete and concise sentences.

3. Activities

Geography

The last question on the comprehension page is usually a map exercise. The map locations focus on Mesopotamia, The Holy Land, and Egypt. Surrounding bodies of water and land are also emphasized. Students often learn locations on small maps and fail to understand where the locations are in context. It is very important to use globes and world maps to make sure students know where Mesopotamia, The Holy Land, and Egypt are in relationship to Europe, Africa, Arabia, etc. Locations are repeated throughout the lessons.

Picture Review

The Teacher Manual includes a picture review section with answers for each lesson. The Picture Review can be done immediately after reading the story, along with the Comprehension Questions, or as a fun review at the end of the lesson. Finding details in pictures is enjoyable for students and helps to reinforce learning.

Other Activities
Other activities include art, drawing the temple, family trees, timelines, etc. Timelines and family trees are very difficult and should be done on the board by the teacher with input from students. Children love to draw and are inspired by the dramatic stories in the Bible. Our Memoria Press composition books are a useful resource for teachers. Students can copy their memory verse on the right-hand page and draw a picture on the left-hand page.

Memory Verse

Introduce the Memory Verse early in the week so students will have the whole week to master it. Read the memory verse to students and explain vocabulary, concepts, and significance.

There are no lines for answers in this section. In order to save time, answer questions orally, or allow students to jot down answers without complete sentences. Give maximum time to mastering the memory verse rather than writing neat answers, but be sure students understand the memory verse first.

Do not ask students to memorize the memory verse independently. Instead, use the *Disappearing Verse Technique* to teach each new verse in class. Write the verse on the board and recite the whole verse together several times. Break the verse down into small sections. Have students recite one section together, and then erase that section. Pointing to the "erased" section on the board, ask students, individually and then in unison, to recite what you erased. Repeat until the whole verse has been erased from the board. As a final exercise, students should stand and recite the verse as a class or independently with poise and perfection. Require students to learn the book of the memory verse but not the complete reference.

Memory verses in this study guide were carefully chosen because they convey vivid images of events and people in Salvation History. Because of their beauty, poetic qualities, and significance, they are memorable and are frequently alluded to in great literature. Many, in fact, are good art or composition prompts. Memory verses that are adult favorites, but more doctrinal and abstract, are not age-appropriate and have been avoided in this program.

Memory verses from the *Memoria Press Copybooks 1-3* have been included in Appendix I of this manual and the Student Text. The verses are numbered for easy reference. The first 27 verses correspond to stories in this text and will be referenced in the appropriate lesson.

Students who have learned these verses will enjoy reviewing them. A major goal of the *Memoria Press Christian Studies* program for K-6 is to review the memory verses on a regular schedule every year so that they enter the students' permanent memory and become a life-long treasure. Students who have not used the *Copybooks* will enjoy exposure to them as well.

Review and Recitation

Every lesson should begin with a few minutes of "rapid-fire" review. Students like a *quick* review of what they already know. They love to answer questions that cover the whole range of learning for the year. It is a great motivation for them to learn more when they realize how much they have learned. **The Facts to Know** easily translate into good quick review questions. Give the word in the left-hand column and ask, "who or what." Or give the definition in the right-hand column and ask, "who or what." **Picture Review** can also be used during review time. Select pictures and ask, "who, what, or when." **Memory Verses** should be reviewed in a cumulative manner all year. Review each verse five weeks in a row after it is introduced, and then periodically thereafter. Give students the first word or two and see if they can complete the verse.
Bees and games are a motivational and fun way to review.

Books of the Old Testament

Students should be able to recite the books of the Bible in order and be familiar with the content of each book. The books of the Old Testament will be learned in *Christian Studies I* and reviewed in *II* and *III*. The books of the New Testament will be learned in *Christian Studies III*. Some children already know the books of the Bible from Sunday School, but many do not.

Canon of the Old Testament

In addition to the 39 books of the Hebrew Old Testament that are accepted by all Christian churches, there are seven "deuterocanonical" books, most likely written in Aramaic, that are included in Catholic and Eastern Orthodox Bibles. These books are found in historic bibles such as the Greek Septuagint and the Latin Vulgate, and even though they are considered apocryphal (disputed) by Protestants, they are important documents for the study of Israel and the church; for this reason, students should learn them. Latin students will encounter the deuterocanon when they begin Latin translation with the Vulgate.

Memoria Press products are designed to be used by all Trinitarian Christians. Our policy is to focus on the things that unite us and leave the divisive topics to be addressed by parents at home. If you are a homeschooler or are teaching in a religiously affiliated school, you may teach or omit these books in accordance with your beliefs. However, for teachers in a non-denominational school, the canon of Scripture presents a problem. Because grammar school children are not ready to deal with religious differences in a classroom setting, you should teach the 39 books of the Hebrew Bible in class and avoid discussion of differences in the Biblical canon. Thirty-nine books are quite enough to learn in one year and they fit the 5-12-5-5-12 scheme. Catholic and Eastern Orthodox families can teach the seven books of the Aramaic canon at home or they can wait until the 7th grade, where they are included in our 7th grade Christian Studies. At this time, students are advised to consult their parents or pastor about their status.

The deuterocanonical books are Tobit, Judith, I Maccabees, II Maccabees, Wisdom, Sirach, and Baruch.

Teaching Instructions for Books of the Bible

Write a selection of books on the board. Pronounce each one slowly, breaking it down into distinct exaggerated syllables. Have students repeat after you. Point out phonetic and non-phonetic spellings. Tell a little about each book and write out "subtitles" on the board to help students remember what each book is about. (The remaining subtitles will be added next year.) Lead the class in two or three oral recitations of the books. Make sure each student can pronounce each book. Then use the *Disappearing Verse Technique* as described in the Teaching Guidelines. Finish by asking students to write each book three times.

The books of the Hebrew Old Testament can be divided into five categories:

Law	5 books
History	12 books
Wisdom	5 books
Major Prophets	5 books
Minor Prophets	12 books

Teach students to remember 5-12-5-5-12 as you introduce each new section of books.

Law	Genesis, Exodus, Leviticus, Numbers, Deuteronomy
History	Joshua, Judges, Ruth, I II Samuel, I II Kings, I II Chronicles, Ezra, Nehemiah, Esther
Wisdom	Job, Psalms, Proverbs, Ecclesiastes, Song of Solomon
Major Prophets	Isaiah, Jeremiah, Lamentations, Ezekiel, Daniel
Minor Prophets	Hosea, Joel, Amos, Obadiah, Jonah, Micah, Nahum, Habakkuk, Zephaniah, Haggai, Zechariah, Malachi

The books that are to be taught each week are listed in the teaching guidelines of each lesson, beginning in Lesson 6.

- Lesson 6: Genesis, Exodus, Leviticus, Numbers, Deuteronomy
- Lesson 7: Joshua, Judges, Ruth
- Lesson 8: I & II Samuel, I & II Kings, I & II Chronicles
- Lesson 9: Ezra, Nehemiah, Esther
- Lesson 13: Job, Psalms, Proverbs, Ecclesiastes, Song of Solomon
- Lesson 16: Isaiah, Jeremiah, Lamentations, Ezekiel, Daniel
- Lesson 18: Hosea, Joel, Amos, Obadiah
- Lesson 19: Jonah, Micah, Nahum, Habakkuk
- Lesson 20: Zephaniah, Haggai, Zechariah, Malachi

Lesson 1

Background and Summary

The first three chapters of Genesis are some of the most beautiful, poetic, and profound passages in the Bible.

The Bible is the only ancient work that describes the origin of the universe as the work of a creator God who is pre-existent to, and outside of, the material world. Genesis also gives the "how" of creation: God speaks it into existence. Both of these are profound insights that are unique to Scripture.

Secondly, the origin of man and his relationship to the Creator and Creation are clearly defined: man is made in the image of God and is God's representative in the creation; therefore man is given dominion over it. In addition, if man is God's image, he must have reason and free will, which is illustrated by the forbidden fruit of the Tree of Knowledge of Good and Evil.

This is a long lesson. You may want to spend two weeks on it.

Selected Reading:
Psalm 8

Facts to Know

Creation	God made everything "out of nothing"
ex nihilo	Latin for 'out of nothing'
Garden of Eden	where God placed man to enjoy life
Mesopotamia	"land between the rivers" (Tigris and Euphrates Rivers)
Iraq	modern-day Mesopotamia
Tree of Knowledge of Good and Evil	tree in middle of Garden of Eden; God said not to eat of it
Euphrates	one of the four branches of the river flowing out of Eden
Imago Dei	Latin for "the image of God"

Memory Verse

Genesis 1:26-28
And God said, Let us make man in our image, after our likeness; and let them have dominion over the fish of the sea and over the fowl of the air and over all the earth. So God created man in His own image, in the image of God created He him; male and female created He them. And God blessed them, and God said unto them, Be fruitful, and multiply, and replenish the earth, and subdue it.

1. What is an image? How is man like God?
   When you look in a mirror, you see an image (a representation) of yourself. Man is the image of God in creation. Man is like God in that he has 1) dominion and 2) reason.
2. What is dominion? Who has ultimate dominion over the earth? Who did God choose to rule the earth and all of the animals in it for Him?
   Dominion means power or rule. God has ultimate dominion because He created the earth. Man, meaning humans, male and female, is to rule the earth in God's place, promoting His will. (p. 15)
3. What command did God give to the man and woman after creating and blessing them? What does this command mean?
   God said, "Be fruitful and multiply and fill the earth." This command means to have children and fill the earth with people in order to rule it and bring it under the power of man, who is God's representative on earth.

4

Vocabulary and Expressions

1. **ex nihilo** (ex **nee** il loh): *Latin*, out of nothing
2. **imago Dei** (ee **mah** goh **day** ee): *Latin*, image of God
3. **dominion**: power; rule, *from the Latin* **Dominus**, Lord or master
4. **fowl**: bird
5. **replenish**: to restock; to fill
6. **subdue**: to control; to tame

The Garden of Eden   Genesis 1-2

Comprehension Questions

1. What was Adam's responsibility in the Garden of Eden? Did he have to grow his own food?
God told Adam to "dress" (tend) and keep the garden. The plants and trees provided food freely, without cultivation or weeds. (pp. 15, 16)

2. Give the names of the two special trees in the middle of the garden.
The Tree of Life; the Tree of Knowledge of Good and Evil. (p. 16)

3. What was the difference between the two trees?
Adam and Eve could eat of the Tree of Life, for it provided food for eternal life. God told Adam and Eve to not eat of the Tree of Knowledge of Good and Evil, for if they did they would die. (p. 16)

4. Why did God bring all of the animals to Adam?
God brought the animals to Adam so he could name them and to see if any of them could be a companion for him. (p. 19)

5. How did God make woman?
God put man into a deep sleep, and then He took one of Adam's ribs and made Woman. (p. 19)

6. What did Adam say when God brought him the woman?
"This is now bone of my bones and flesh of my flesh. She shall be called Woman because she was taken out of Man."

7. Find on 1) globe or world map, and 2) Unit I Map A:

☐ Mesopotamia (Iraq)   ☐ Euphrates River   ☐ Tigris River

8. Memorize the 7 days of Creation.

5

Activities

pp. 14-15   Identify the picture that represents each day of the Creation.

pp. 16-17   Describe the Garden of Eden. Identify what might be the Tree of Knowledge of Good and Evil.

pp. 18-19   Look at the picture of the Garden of Eden. Name the animals you see. What do you notice about the relationship between the animals?

The animals are peaceful. The lion and tiger do not attack the deer or the sheep. Adam may be naming the animals.

Memory Verse Review: #1-7 in Appendix. Give the first word or two of a verse and see how many students can complete it.

Lesson 2

Background and Summary

In the Garden of Eden, man is in a perfect state of harmony with God and creation. But Satan, the Father of Lies, deceives Eve, and she and Adam disobey God's simple command to refrain from eating the forbidden fruit. In this way, sin enters the world. Man is separated from God, fallen from his original perfection, and now experiences sorrow all the days of his life. Help the students understand that, more than breaking a rule, Adam and Eve radically disrupted the order of creation. Man was meant to rule the earth under God's authority, not reject it for his own pleasures.

God's punishment, however, is not without a promise of hope. The memory verse for this lesson contains a mysterious prophecy about the war between Satan and humanity, and a future defeat for Satan. The account of humanity's first children, Cain and Abel, and the moral tragedy that took place between them, further heightens the anticipation of a promised seed (Jesus, the Son of Man) that will triumph over the evil one.

Selected Readings:
- **Romans 16:20** for the Battle of the Seeds.
- **Romans 5:12** for Original Sin, the effect of Adam's sin upon humanity.
- **Romans 5:18-19** for Christ as the Second Adam, the head of a new race: the renewed, righteous humanity.

Facts to Know

Serpent	a snake; the most cunning beast that tempted Eve
Forbidden Fruit	fruit of the **Tree of Knowledge of Good and Evil**
Tree of Life	in the middle of the Garden of Eden, a flaming sword guarded the path to it
The Fall of Man	the sin of Adam and Eve which caused the fall of the human race from its original state of perfection
cherubim	an order of angels
Cain and Abel	Adam and Eve's first sons
Seth	Adam and Eve's third son

Memory Verse

Genesis 3:14-15
And the Lord God said unto the serpent, Because thou hast done this, thou art cursed above every beast of the field. And I will put enmity between thee and the woman, and between thy seed and her seed; it shall bruise thy head, and thou shalt bruise his heel.

1. In verse 14, what physical curse did God give the serpent?
   God cursed the serpent so that he had to crawl on his belly and eat dust all of his days.

2. What is "seed"? Who is the seed of woman?
   Seed is offspring or children. Christ is the seed of woman.

3. What is enmity? What is the spiritual curse of the serpent?
   Enmity is similar to enemy. It means conflict or discord. The serpent is the enemy of the woman's offspring—the whole human race and Christ.

4. How did the seed of the woman bruise the head of the serpent?
   The serpent and his seed have brought sin and death into the world, but Christ defeated the serpent when his resurrection destroyed the power of death.

5. How did the serpent bruise his heel?
   The serpent (the devil) instigated the plot that brought about the death of Christ.

6

Vocabulary and Expressions

1. **subtil**: *King James Bible language for* subtle (See Verse 8 in Appendix 1).
2. **cunning**: clever; crafty
3. **enmity**: ill will; opposite of friendship; enemies
4. **forbidden fruit**: what Adam and Eve could not eat
5. **"For dust thou art, and unto dust shalt thou return"** (Gen. 3:19): Man comes from creation and in death returns to creation (containing an implied separation between the realm of heaven and the realm of earth).
6. **"A fugitive and a vagabond shalt thou be upon the earth"**: Cain was cursed to wander the earth without a home.

Cain and Abel   Genesis 3-6

Comprehension Questions

1. How did the serpent tempt Eve to disobey God?

   The serpent (the devil) mixed a truth with a lie and deceived Eve. He said she would not die if she ate of the tree, a lie, and he said she would be like God in knowing good and evil, the truth.

2. What is the Fall of Man, and what were its consequences?

   The Fall of Man is when Adam and Eve sinned and fell from their original perfection and favor with God. Their children and the whole human race suffer the effects of their fall.

3. What happened after Adam and Eve ate the forbidden fruit?

   Their eyes were opened. They knew they were naked and they sewed fig leaves together to cover themselves. No longer were they innocent before God.

4. Why did Adam and Eve hide themselves when God "walked in the garden in the cool of the day"? They were afraid because they had disobeyed God.

5. How did God curse Adam? Eve? What did that mean for the human race?

   Adam would have to "work by the sweat of his brow" to provide food for his family, because the ground would now resist his authority by bringing forth weeds, thorns, and thistles. Eve would suffer pain in childbirth and her husband would rule over her. Both man and woman would have sorrow, which was not known before, all the days of their lives, and would return to dust when they died.

6. What work did Cain do? What work did Abel do?

   Cain grew food, "tilled the ground." Abel was a shepherd, a keeper of sheep. They represent the two sources of food for humans.

7. Who was a ninth generation descendant of Adam?

   Noah was the ninth descendant of Adam.

8. Find on 1) globe or world map, and 2) Unit I Map A: ☐ Mesopotamia (Iraq)

   ☐ Tigris and Euphrates Rivers   ☐ Red Sea   ☐ Persian Gulf   ☐ Arabia

7

Picturing the Truth

For each picture, help the students understand the important lessons about God behind the story.

- God is a comforter to the downtrodden.
- God is a holy and just judge over His creation.
- God's warnings must be taken seriously.

Activities

pp. 20-21   Where is the serpent? What is Eve doing?
The serpent is in the tree. Eve is giving the forbidden fruit to Adam.

pp. 22-23   What are Adam and Eve doing? What are they wearing? Who made their clothes?
Adam and Eve are being driven from the garden. God made their clothes out of animal skins.

pp. 24-25   Identify Cain and Abel and what they are doing in all three pictures.
On p. 24 Cain is plowing, tilling the ground, and Abel is tending his sheep. At the top of p. 25, Abel is giving his pleasing sacrifice to God, and Cain is looking on with jealousy. On the bottom of p. 25, Cain has killed Abel.

Memory Verse Review: #8-13 in Appendix. Give the first word or two of a verse and see how many students can complete it.

Lesson 3

Background and Summary

The genealogies of Genesis continue to anticipate a promised seed that will defeat the seed of the serpent. Unfortunately, by the time of Noah, the seed of the serpent appears to have dominion! Man becomes so evil that the "imagination of his heart was evil continually." God responds to the increasing wickedness of man by judging the earth with a flood and restarting the creation project with a righteous family, the house of Noah.

The agreement between God and Noah, symbolized by the rainbow, is the first of many instances of God's covenant with His people in Salvation History.

Salvation History is the history of God's redemption of man from his fallen state of sin and separation from God. The first 11 chapters of Genesis detail the fall of man (the problem). The rest of the Bible focuses upon God's plan of redemption (the solution).

Selected Reading:
Hebrews 11:7 for the obedient faith of Noah.

Facts to Know

Noah	the only righteous man on earth; built the Ark
Great Flood	destroyed all living things on Earth
Rainbow	symbol of God's covenant with man
Tower of Babel	where God confused language
Shem, Ham, Japheth	Noah's sons
Ararat	mountain where Ark came to rest
covenant	God's promise; a binding agreement

Memory Verse

How many of these Copybook verses do you remember?

1. But Noah found grace in the eyes of the Lord. Noah was a just man and perfect in his generation and Noah walked with God. And Noah begat three sons, Shem, Ham and Japheth. - Genesis 6:8-10

2. Make thee an ark of gopher wood. - Genesis 6:14

3. And the rain was upon the earth forty days and forty nights. - Genesis 7:12

4. I do set my bow in the cloud, and it shall be for a token of a covenant between me and the earth. - Genesis 9:13

8

Vocabulary and Expressions

1. **gopher wood**: The King James Bible, the source for our memory verses, uses the term *gopher wood*, and the *GCB* identifies the tree as a cypress.
2. **"Let us make a name for ourselves"**: In Old Testament times, names were very significant, as we will soon see. The people of Babel wanted to establish a reputation for themselves above all names. Only God can have supreme glory, a name above all names.

The Tower of Babel   Genesis 6-11

Comprehension Questions

1. Why did God decide to destroy all living things on Earth?

   God saw that mankind had become very wicked, and their minds and hearts were evil. God regretted that he had made man and decided to end all flesh. (p. 26)

2. Who and what was to be admitted onto Noah's Ark?

   Noah, his wife, and his three sons and their wives were allowed on the ark, along with two of each living creature (male and female) and some of every kind of food. (p. 26)

3. How long did it rain? How long was the Great Flood upon the earth?

   It rained for 40 days and 40 nights. (p. 28)

   The flood was on the earth for 150 days. (Gen. 7:24)

4. How did Noah know that the water had dried from the earth?

   Noah sent out a dove three times to see if the waters had dried. The first time the dove returned, the second time she returned with an olive leaf, and the third time she did not return at all. So Noah knew the earth was dry. (pp. 30-31)

5. What promise did God make to man and every living creature on Earth after the flood?

   He promised that never again would all flesh be cut off by the waters of the flood nor would a flood destroy the earth. (p. 31)

6. Why did God confuse language so that men could not understand one another?

   God thought that if the people had only one language, nothing would restrain them from doing whatever they conceived. (p. 32)

7. Find on 1) globe or world map, and 2) Unit I Map A: ☐ Mesopotamia (Iraq)

   ☐ Tigris and Euphrates Rivers ☐ Red Sea ☐ Persian Gulf ☐ Arabia

   ☐ Africa ☐ Egypt ☐ Mt. Ararat ☐ Mediterranean Sea

9

Teacher Notes

1. The rain was upon the earth 40 days, but the flood was on the earth 150 days (Gen. 7:24). Scripture says that the fountains of the great deep were broken up and the windows of heaven were opened (Gen. 7:11). In other words, water came from above and below. The great streams of water under the earth also contributed to the flood in a great cataclysmic event.

2. There are many flood stories in world mythologies, the most famous being the one from Greek mythology. Such widespread accounts of a great flood are strong evidence that it was a real event, rather than a myth.

3. According to *D'Aulaires' Book of Greek Myths* (pp. 76-77), Prometheus knew that Zeus was planning to flood the earth, so he warned his son Deucalion to build an ark in order to survive. After Zeus sent nine days of constant rain, Deucalion and his wife, Pyrrha, emerged from their ark on the tenth day to find the earth desolate and empty of life. Glad to have survived themselves, Deucalion and Pyrrha thanked the gods. For their piety, Zeus rewarded them with the ability to repopulate the earth with a new race of "rock-solid people."

4. Bible stories are sober and realistic. Although they describe miraculous events, they never contain the fantastical elements found in Greek and other mythologies (e.g., the formation of the "rock people.")

Activities

pp. 27-27 Identify Noah and the Ark. Who built Noah's Ark?
Noah's family, including his three sons (Shem, Ham and Japheth), built the ark.

pp. 28-29 How many animals can you identify?
Deer, cattle, lions, a rhinoceros, a hippo, giraffes, elephants, monkeys, goats, and a lamb.

pp. 30-31 What is Noah doing at the top of the page? What does the dove have in its beak?
Noah is letting out a dove to see if there is dry land. The dove has an olive leaf in its beak.

pp. 30 Where is the ark? How many animals can you identify?
The ark came to rest on Mt. Ararat. Camel, deer, ostrich, lion, tiger, snake, elephant, giraffe, fox, cow, sheep, rabbit, goat, bear, bird.

pp. 32-33 What are the people doing, and why?
The people of Babel are making bricks and building a tower, in order to reach Heaven.

What is the story of the Great Flood according to Greek Mythology? Compare and contrast the Bible and pagan flood stories. See Teacher Notes above.

Lesson 4

Background and Summary

The Bible's account of Abraham centers on the significance of God's promise to make a people for himself (Gen. 12-24). We see the truly gracious nature of God's covenant with His people in the fact that God's calling of Abram precludes any merit on the part of the recipient (Gen. 12). God extends a twofold blessing to Abram by both calling him to the land of his inheritance and promising the childless man to become father of a great nation.

The story of Abram remains an amazing lesson about faith. God called Abram to leave his family and home and make a journey to a new land. He was not able to see the land first. He had to walk by faith, not by sight. He learned how to hold onto God's promises in the midst of uncertain times. Thus, Abraham is a model for all of us. We, too, walk by faith on life's journey. We cannot see where we are going, but God can.

Selected Readings:
- **Hebrews 11:8-10** for the faith of Abraham.
- **Galatians 3:9** also for the faith of Abraham and those that follow his example of faith in trusting Christ.
- **Acts 7:2-8** for Stephen's summary of Abraham.

Facts to Know

Abraham	father of many nations; father of the faithful
Sarah	wife of Abraham
Lot	Abraham's nephew
Canaan	land given to Abraham
Call of Abraham	2000 B.C.

Memory Verse

Genesis 12:1-3   The Call of Abraham

Now the Lord said unto Abram, Get thee out of thy country and from thy kindred and from thy Father's house, unto a land that I will shew thee; And I will make of thee a great nation and I will bless thee, and in thee all the families of the Earth shall be blessed.

1. What is "kindred"?   relatives; family

2. What word could be used instead of "shew"?   show

3. What land did God promise to Abraham?   Canaan

4. How were all of the families of the earth blessed through Abraham?

   Abraham was the father of the faithful—those who followed God.

10

Vocabulary and Expressions

1. **country**: ethnic nationality or people group
2. **kindred**: tribe or clan; relatives
3. **house**: parents; brothers; close relatives

Help students remember the order of these three words in this verse. Country, kindred, and house are progressively smaller and more closely related peoples.

Abram and Lot   Genesis 12-17

Comprehension Questions

1. Where was Abram living when God asked him to leave his home? How old was he?
   Abram lived in Haran and was 75 when God called him to leave. Abram's father, Terah, and his family were born in Ur in Mesopotamia before moving to Haran. (p. 34)

2. Who did Abram take with him on his journey?
   Abram took his wife, Sarai, and his brother's son, Lot, on the journey. He also took all their goods, cattle, and servants they had gathered in Haran. (p. 34)

3. Why did Abram and Lot separate? What land did each choose? Who got first choice?
   The herdsmen of Abram and Lot were fighting, and the land was not large enough to support both of them. Abraham gave Lot first choice of the land. Lot chose the plain of Jordan. Abram lived in Canaan. Lot pitched his tent toward Sodom and Abram in the Plain of Mamre, in Hebron. This is significant in that Lot moved toward Sodom, a wicked, sinful city, while Abram chose land in the opposite direction, which God intended, and built an altar to the Lord. (p. 36)

4. What promises did God make to Abram?
   The Lord promised that Sarai would have a son and that Abram's descendants would be as numerous as the dust of the earth and the stars in the heavens. His children would have the land of Canaan for their inheritance forever.

5. What new names did God give Abram and Sarai?
   Abraham and Sarah were the names chosen. (p. 39)

6. Find on Unit 1 Map A: ☐ Ur of the Chaldees ☐ Canaan ☐ Haran

   Find on Unit 1 Map B: ☐ Bethel ☐ Shechem ☐ Hebron (Plain of Mamre)

   ☐ Sea of Galilee ☐ Mediterranean Sea ☐ Dead Sea

11

Patriarch Family Tree

Adam and Eve

Cain & Abel   *Seth*

Noah

Shem   Ham Japheth

Terah

Abram

Activities

Draw a family tree that includes: Adam and Eve, Cain, Abel, Seth, Noah, Shem, Ham, Japheth, Terah, and Abram. Students cannot do this as an assignment. It should be a teacher-directed activity.

pp. 34-35   Identify Abram. With your finger, trace his journey on *The Golden Children's Bible* map and also on the Review Lesson map.

pp. 36-37   Identify Abram and Lot. What are they discussing? Who are the men in the background, and what are they doing?
Abram and Lot are dividing the land. The men in the background are their herdsmen, who are fighting over the land.

Memory Verse Review: #18 in Appendix. Give the first word or two of a verse and see how many students can complete it.

Hagar and Ishmael (Genesis 16)

For ten years Abram lived in Canaan, and his wife, Sarai, bore him no children. Sarai had an Egyptian maid called Hagar. Sarai said to Abram, "The Lord has not allowed me to bear children. Go to my maid, so that I may obtain children by her." And Abram did as Sarai said.

Sarai gave Hagar to Abram as a wife. But when Hagar realized that she was with Abram's child, she began to despise Sarai. To Sarai's complaint, Abram said, "Hagar is your maid, do with her as you please." So Sarai dealt harshly with Hagar, who then fled into the wilderness.

The Lord found Hagar by a fountain and asked, "Where have you come from and where are you going?" When she replied that she had fled from her mistress, the Lord told her to go back to Sarai and submit.

The Lord reassured her, "You will have many children. The child you now carry will be a son, whom you shall call Ishmael, meaning 'God that hears,' because I have heard your suffering. This son will be a wild man, who will dwell among his brethren, although he will fight with them and they will fight with him." And Hagar bore Abram a son, Ishmael, when Abram was 86 years old.

Abraham Pleads with God (Genesis 18)

After the Three Angels had announced the impending birth of Isaac to Abraham and Sarah, they departed for Sodom and Gomorrah to see how wicked those cities had become. As Abraham walked with the angels to send them off, they told him of their intention to judge those cities. Through an angel, the Lord said, "The outcry of Sodom and Gomorrah is indeed great, and their sin is very grave."

As two of the angels departed for Sodom and Gomorrah, Abraham remembered his relatives there and began to plead with the Lord, saying, "Will you indeed destroy the righteous with the wicked? Suppose that there are fifty righteous people left there, will you spare the place for those fifty?"

The Lord answered Abraham and said, "If I find fifty righteous people in the city, then I will spare it." Then Abraham humbled himself before the Lord and said, "Now I have been bold to speak to the Lord even though I am but dust and ashes. Suppose the fifty righteous lack five? Or suppose only forty righteous are found there?" And again he wondered, "May the Lord not be angry with me, suppose thirty are found there? Or suppose only twenty are found there?" Finally, Abraham asked, "Will you destroy the city if only ten righteous people are found there?"

Each time Abraham asked, the Lord responded in mercy to his prayer. He agreed to Abraham's request and said, "I will not destroy the place on account of ten." When they finished speaking, the Lord departed, and Abraham returned home.

Lot's Wife; Sodom and Gomorrah (Genesis 19)

One evening, two angels came to Sodom, where Lot went to live after he separated from his uncle Abram. Lot of Sodom rose to meet them. With his face toward the ground, Lot offered them the hospitality of his house for the night. They said they would spend the night in the street, but Lot insisted, and they gave in.

Lot made them a dinner of unleavened bread. Before the angels could retire for the night, people from all quarters of the city, young and old, came to the house asking to see the visitors. They said to Lot, "Bring these men out so we can see who they are."

Lot went out, closing the door behind him. He said, "Do not act so wickedly. I have two unmarried daughters I will bring out for you to see, but do not disturb these men who have taken shelter under my roof." The mob threatened Lot and moved toward the door, as if to break it down.

The angels reached out and pulled Lot inside. Then they made every member of the mob blind. The angels told Lot, "If you have any other family in this city, take them out, because the Lord is tired of hearing all the cries of these people and has sent us to destroy the city."

Lot went out to his sons-in-law and the daughters whom they had married. "Get out of this place," he told them, "because the Lord is going to destroy it." But they thought he was crazy.

When morning came, the angels told Lot to hurry, to take his wife and the two daughters living in the house, and leave before they were consumed with the city. He lingered, so the angels took his hand and the hands of his wife and daughters and transported them outside the city. The angels told them, "Flee for your lives. Do not look back. Do not stay in the plain. Escape to the mountain or you will be destroyed."

Lot said, "I cannot. I appreciate the mercy you have shown me, but I fear the mountain. Let me escape to the little town of Zoar, where I am not afraid to live." The angels allowed this and promised not to destroy Zoar.

It was midday when Lot entered Zoar, and the Lord rained fire and brimstone upon Sodom and the neighboring city of Gomorrah. These two cities were completely destroyed, along with all their inhabitants and everything that grew in the surrounding plain. Lot's wife looked back at the spectacle and became a pillar of salt.

Abraham was up early that morning and saw the smoke from the destruction of Sodom and Gomorrah. God had remembered his promise to take care of Abraham, and for this reason, had arranged to save Abraham's nephew, Lot. After witnessing the violent events and seeing his wife turned to salt, Lot thought better of staying in Zoar, and took his daughters to the mountain, where they all lived together in a cave. Later, Lot's two daughters bore sons, one named Moab, who became the father of the Moabites, and another, who became the father of the Ammonites. Both groups would later oppose the nation of Israel.

Lesson 5

Background and Summary

Hagar and Ishmael: God repeatedly promises Abraham that he will be the father of a great nation and that his children will be numberless, but by Genesis 16 he and Sarah have still not had any children! Again, Abraham's faith is put to the test. In this story, Sarah decides to "take matters into her own hands" and give her handmaid to Abraham, so they can have a son. Her good intentions, however, do not coincide with God's perfect plan and result in a lasting conflict between the descendants of Isaac (son of Abraham and Sarah) and the descendants of Ishmael (son of Abraham and Hagar).

Like Sarah, we, too, are impatient and lose faith when things don't happen as quickly as we think they should. This is a very human reaction. We panic and end up making a mess of things. God wants to teach us to depend on Him more through the waiting times.

The Three Angels: When visited by three angels on the plains of Mamre, Sarah cannot help but laugh at the message that she will bear Abraham a son in her old age. Yet God, despite her lack of faith, rewards her with a child to be named Isaac, which means "laughter" (Gen. 21). In this way, the Lord gets the last laugh, since the old man and woman who laughed in disbelief soon laugh with joy at the birth of the promised son (Gen. 21:6-7).

Selected Readings:
* **Genesis 17:17** for Abraham's laughing when God told him he would have a son in his old age.
* **Galatians 4:28-31** for Paul's connection of Isaac, the child of promise, with those who are sons of God through faith in Christ.

Facts to Know

Hagar	handmaid of Sarah; mother of Ishmael
Ishmael	son of Abraham and Hagar; father of Ishmaelites
Sodom and Gomorrah	wicked cities destroyed by fire and brimstone
Lot's wife	turned to a pillar of salt
Isaac	Abraham and Sarah's son, whose name means "he who laughs"
Fire and Brimstone	God's punishment for sin

Memory Verse

Genesis 13:12   And Lot pitched his tent toward Sodom.

Genesis 19:26   But Lot's wife looked back, and she became a pillar of salt.

1. What does the expression "Lot pitched his tent toward Sodom" mean? What lesson does that teach us?
   Lot chose to live in the plains when he and Abraham separated. He moved closer and closer to the wicked cities of Sodom and Gomorrah rather than moving away from evil influences.
2. What message did the two angels bring to Lot?
   God was going to destroy the wicked cities of Sodom and Gomorrah and he should leave with his family.
3. How did Abraham try to save Sodom and Gomorrah?
   He asked God to spare them if he could find ten righteous men in the place.
4. Why was Lot's wife punished? What lesson does that teach us?
   Lot's wife was punished because she looked back on the life of sin in the city rather than looking forward to her future salvation from sin. To follow God without looking back is the lesson we should take from this story.

14

Teacher Notes

The spiritual application of the story of Lot's wife is that we will die spiritually if we look back with longing toward sin rather than forward to a future free from sin.

The spiritual application of Lot pitching his tent toward Sodom is that if we move toward evil influences, we will not be able to resist the temptations and will eventually be ensnared in a life of sin.

The Three Angels   Genesis 16-19

Comprehension Questions

1. Why did Sarah drive her handmaid away?

   Hagar became haughty when she knew she was going to have Abraham's child.

2. How did God comfort Hagar?

   God found her in the wilderness and told her to go back and submit to Sarah and that she would have many children.

3. What kind of man did God say Ishmael would be?

   He would be a wild man and a fighter.

4. What message did the three angels bring to Abraham?

   The angels told Abraham that he and Sarah would have a son.

5. What was Sarah's reaction?

   Sarah laughed to herself.

6. What does Isaac mean?   Isaac means "he who laughs."

7. How old were Sarah and Abraham when Isaac was born?

   Abraham was 100; Sarah was 90. (p. 39)

8. What did Abraham do when he learned of the angels' intention to judge Sodom and Gomorrah?

   Abraham prayed to God to have mercy on his relatives living in Sodom.

9. How were the wicked cities of Sodom and Gomorrah destroyed by God?

   God judged the wicked cities of the valley by raining fire and brimstone on the land.

10. Find on Unit 1 Map B: ☐ Bethel   ☐ Shechem   ☐ Hebron (Plain of Mamre)

    ☐ Dead Sea   ☐ Sodom and Gomorrah   ☐ Jordan River

15

Activities

pp. 40-41   Identify Abraham, Sarah, the three guests. Who were the guests? What did they tell Abraham? What is Abraham doing? What is Sarah doing?

The guests are angels sent from God to tell Abraham that he and Sarah are going to have a son. Abraham is serving the three guests food, cakes that Sarah had baked. Sarah is laughing to herself because she heard them say that she would have a child.

Draw a picture of the following:

Sarah laughing at the thought of bearing a child.
Sodom and Gomorrah destroyed by fire and brimstone.
Lot's wife who was turned into a pillar of salt.

Review Lesson: Unit 1

Instructions

Use this Review Lesson to support mastery of the material presented in the previous five lessons. Drill the Facts to Know orally or have a Facts to Know Bee. Places to Know should be identified on the maps in this lesson. Events to Know will be reviewed in the timeline exercise which follows. Students may work independently on these two pages of the Review, but answers should be checked in class. A test for this unit is included in the back of this book.

Review Lesson: Unit 1 (Lessons 1-5)

Salvation History

Periods: Prehistory, The Age of the Patriarchs

Dates:	Prehistory	Time Begins
	The Call of Abraham	2000 B.C.

Prehistory Events
The Creation
The Garden of Eden
The Fall of Man
The First Murder
The Flood
The Tower of Babel

Patriarchs, Events
The Call of Abraham
Pick of the Land
Driven into the Wilderness
Fire and Brimstone
Pillar of Salt
The Child of Promise

People to Know
Adam
Eve
Cain
Abel
Seth
Noah
Shem, Ham, Japheth
Abraham
Sarah
Lot
Lot's wife
Hagar
Ishmael
Isaac

Places to Know
Ur of the Chaldees
Haran
Bethel
Shechem
Hebron
Sodom
Gomorrah
Canaan
Mesopotamia (Iraq)
Arabia
Africa
Egypt
Mt. Ararat
Tigris River
Euphrates River
Jordan River
Persian Gulf
Red Sea
Mediterranean Sea
Dead Sea
Sea of Galilee

Words to Know
imago Dei: image of God
ex nihilo: "out of nothing"
serpent: snake
cherubim: order of angels
covenant: God's promise

Words to Know
dominion: power or rule
cunning: clever; crafty
enmity: ill will
kindred: relatives; tribe
cleave: to join or unite with

What did God create on each of the six days of Creation? On the seventh?

Day One _matter, light and dark; day and night_

Day Two _the air or atmosphere (sky); separated waters above from waters below_

Day Three _dry land, seas, and plants_

Day Four _sun, moon, and stars_

Day Five _animals of seas and air_

Day Six _land animals and humans_

Day Seven _the Sabbath, the day of rest_

16

Geography

Locate on your maps the key points of Abraham's journey. Students can trace with their fingers the route that Abraham took from Ur to Haran to the land of Canaan. This is the Fertile Crescent, the semicircle of fertile land stretching from the coast of the Mediterranean around the Syrian Desert and Arabia and into Mesopotamia.

Although not in *The Golden Children's Bible*, Abraham also went into Egypt for a time.

Review Lesson: Unit 1 (Lessons 1-5)

Give the corresponding word or phrase:

1. Latin for "image of God" _____ Imago Dei
2. Adam and Eve's third son _____ Seth
3. Abraham's nephew _____ Lot
4. Most cunning of beasts _____ serpent
5. Where God placed man to enjoy life _____ Garden of Eden
6. He built the ark _____ Noah
7. Age of Sarah when Isaac was born _____ 90
8. Bird that Noah sent out to find dry land _____ dove
9. Where God confused language _____ Tower of Babel
10. Age of Abraham when Isaac was born _____ 100
11. Tree that God forbade to Adam and Eve _____ Tree of Knowledge of Good and Evil
12. In the Flood, it rained this many days and nights _____ 40
13. Symbol of God's covenant with man _____ rainbow
14. Abraham's wife _____ Sarah
15. "He who laughs" _____ Isaac
16. Adam and Eve's first two sons _____ Cain and Abel
17. The act of bringing the universe into existence _____ Creation
18. Order of angels _____ cherubim
19. Date of Call of Abraham _____ 2000 B.C.
20. Father of many nations _____ Abraham
21. She turned to a pillar of salt _____ Lot's wife
22. Two wicked cities destroyed by fire and brimstone _____ Sodom and Gomorrah
23. Sarah's handmaid; the mother of Ishmael _____ Hagar
24. "Out of nothing" _____ ex nihilo
25. Land given to Abraham as an inheritance _____ Canaan

Match up the vocabulary words:

_C_ dominion   A. relatives; tribe
_B_ cunning   B. crafty or sly
_E_ enmity   C. power or rule
_A_ kindred   D. to join or unite with
_D_ cleave   E. ill will

17

Review Lesson: Unit 1

Old Testament Drill Questions

All of the short answer review questions from each Review Lesson have been compiled in Appendix 2. Continue to review them throughout the year. They are great for bees and competitions.

Review Lesson: Unit 1

Timeline Review

Elementary-age children do not have a well-developed sense of time, especially time long ago and time over a long period. Putting events and people in order is also an advanced skill. These timelines are designed to teach beginning skills in creating a mental timeline of history. Students cannot do this work independently; this is a teacher-directed learning activity. Begin by looking at the Prehistory events and putting them in order; then add them to the timeline. Next, go to the Patriarch events and do the same. Lastly, help students put the people in order and add them to the timeline.

Review Lesson: Unit 1 (Lessons 1-5)

Salvation History Timeline

The events and people of Salvation History are out of order! Put people and events in correct order by numbering 1-10 for People, 1-6 for Prehistory, and 7-12 for the Age of the Patriarchs. Then write dates, periods, events, and people into the timeline chart. For dates and periods, see Review Page.

People to Know
- 6 Abraham and Sarah
- 1 Adam and Eve
- 3 Seth
- 10 Isaac
- 4 Noah
- 2 Cain and Abel
- 8 Hagar and Ishmael
- 5 Shem, Ham, Japheth
- 7 Lot
- 9 Lot's wife

Prehistory Events
- 3 The Fall of Man
- 1 The Creation
- 6 The Tower of Babel
- 5 The Flood
- 2 The Garden of Eden
- 4 The First Murder

The Patriarchs, Events
- 11 Pillar of Salt
- 9 Driven into the Wilderness
- 12 The Child of Promise
- 7 The Call of Abraham
- 8 Pick of the Land
- 10 Fire and Brimstone

Date	Events	Period	People
Time Begins		Prehistory	
	The Creation		
	The Garden of Eden		Adam, Eve
	The Fall of Man		
	The First Murder		Cain and Abel
			Seth
	The Flood		Noah
			Shem, Ham, Japheth
	The Tower of Babel		
2000 B.C.		Patriarchs	
	The Call of Abraham		Abraham
	Pick of the Land		Lot
	Driven into the Wilderness		Hagar and Ishmael
	Fire and Brimstone		
	Pillar of Salt		Lot's wife
	The Child of Promise		Isaac

18

Review Lesson: Unit 1 (Lessons 1-5)

Scripture Memorization

Check each box if you can recite the Scripture verse from memory. Write each from memory or teacher dictation. Be accurate.

☐ **Genesis 1:26-28** _____

And God said, Let us make man in our image, after our likeness; and let them have

dominion over the fish of the sea and over the fowl of the air and over all the earth.

So God created man in His own image, in the image of God created He him; male and

female created He them. And God blessed them, and God said unto them, Be fruitful,

and multiply, and replenish the earth, and subdue it. _____

_____

☐ **Genesis 3:14-15** _____

And the Lord God said unto the serpent, Because thou hast done this, thou art cursed

above every beast of the field. And I will put enmity between thee and the woman, and

between thy seed and her seed; it shall bruise thy head, and thou shalt bruise his heel.

_____

☐ **Genesis 12:1-3** _____

Now the Lord said unto Abram, Get thee out of thy country and from thy kindred and

from thy Father's house, unto a land that I will shew thee; And I will make of thee a great

nation and I will bless thee, and in thee all the families of the Earth shall be blessed.

_____

☐ **Genesis 13:12** _____ And Lot pitched his tent toward Sodom. _____

☐ **Genesis 19:26** _____ But Lot's wife looked back, and she became a pillar of salt.

_____

19

Review Lesson: Unit 1

Memory Verses

To recite memory verses, give the first few words and let students complete the verse orally. Students may write the verse from memory, from dictation, or copy it.

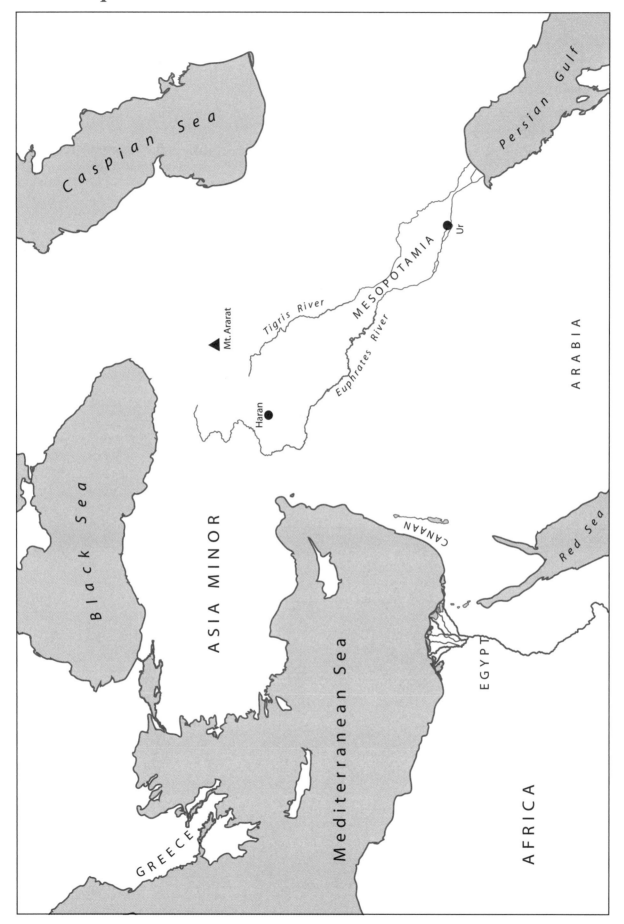

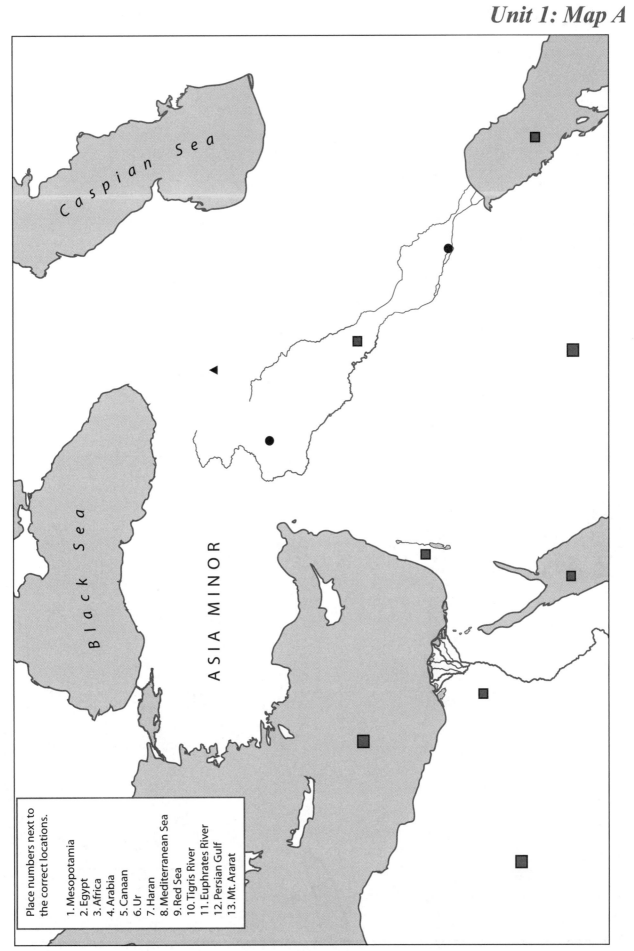

Caspian Sea

Black Sea

ASIA MINOR

Place numbers next to
the correct locations.

1. Mesopotamia
2. Egypt
3. Africa
4. Arabia
5. Canaan
6. Ur
7. Haran
8. Mediterranean Sea
9. Red Sea
10. Tigris River
11. Euphrates River
12. Persian Gulf
13. Mt. Ararat

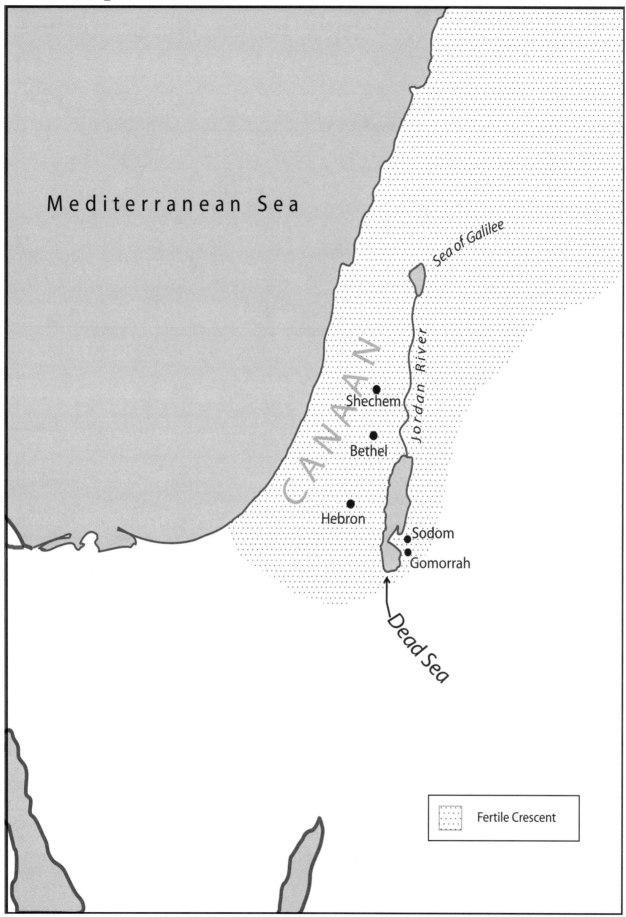

Mediterranean Sea

Sea of Galilee

CANAAN

Jordan River

Shechem

Bethel

Hebron

Sodom

Gomorrah

Dead Sea

Fertile Crescent

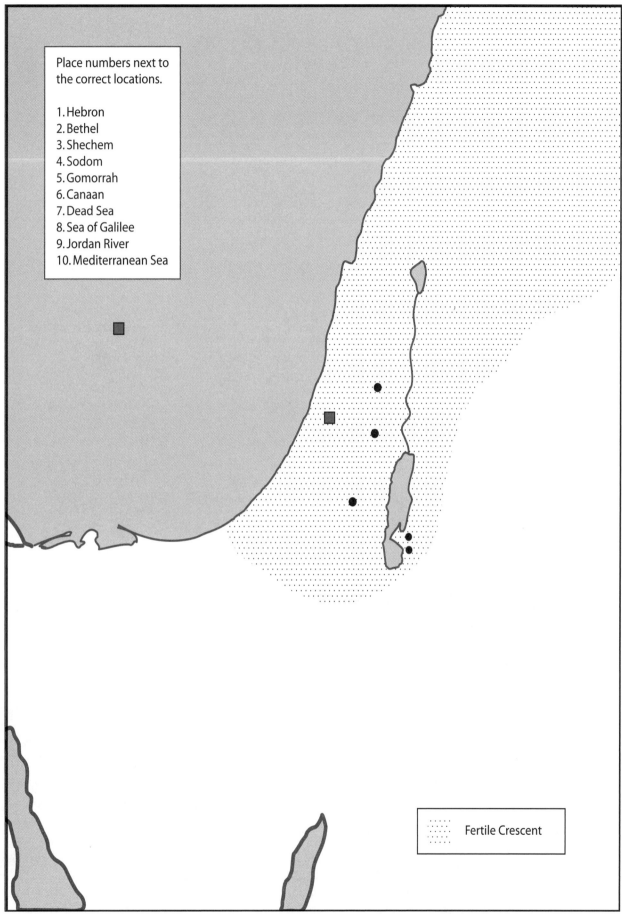

Unit 1: Map B

Place numbers next to the correct locations.

1. Hebron
2. Bethel
3. Shechem
4. Sodom
5. Gomorrah
6. Canaan
7. Dead Sea
8. Sea of Galilee
9. Jordan River
10. Mediterranean Sea

Fertile Crescent

23

The Sacrifice of Isaac (Genesis 22)

After all these things had happened, God tested Abraham. He said to Abraham, "Take your only son, Isaac, whom you love, and offer him as a sacrifice at a place in the mountains that I will point out to you." Abraham got up early the next morning, saddled his donkey, and took his son, Isaac, to the place in the mountains God had shown. He brought wood along for the fire.

He had traveled for three days when he told the two young men he had brought along as helpers to stay behind with the donkey. He said he wanted to worship with his son farther ahead. He gave Isaac the wood to carry, and he himself took fire and a knife.

Isaac said, "I see the wood and the fire, but where is the lamb for the burnt offering?" Abraham said, "God will provide a lamb." When they reached the designated spot, Abraham built an altar. He arranged the wood. He then tied Isaac up and placed him upon the wood on the altar. He picked up the knife and was about to use it to kill his son.

At the last minute, the angel of the Lord called from the sky, "Abraham, Abraham. Do not harm your son. God knows now that your devotion to him is true." As Abraham looked, he saw a ram caught in a thicket by its horns. Abraham took the ram and sacrificed it in place of his son. Abraham called that place Jehovah-jireh, meaning "the Lord will provide," as it was known thereafter.

The angel of the Lord called to Abraham a second time, "Because you were willing to sacrifice your son, the Lord blesses you and guarantees that you shall have more offspring than can be counted. Yours will be the seed for all the nations of the earth, because you have obeyed the Lord."

So Abraham and Isaac returned to the young men, and they all went together to the town of Beersheba, where Abraham lived from then on.

Lesson 6

Background and Summary

In the ancient world, all religions practiced animal sacrifice. People sacrificed the best animals that they had to their gods. Eventually human and child sacrifice became widespread among wicked populations. Baal worship, including human sacrifice, was dominant in the land of Canaan.

Scripture addresses human sacrifice in this story. The lesson is that while an almighty God could require the ultimate sacrifice of a child, the God of Heaven accepts the substitute of a lamb. The meaning of this story becomes complete with Jesus, the Lamb of God. God, in His mercy, sacrifices His own son, rather than asking us to sacrifice our children.

The writer of Hebrews commends the faith of Abraham because he truly relied upon the promise of God for all things, even what he thought was impossible (Hebrews 11:17-19)! In this light, we can see how the story of the attempted sacrifice of Isaac displays beautifully the full-grown faith of Abraham; the "father of multitudes" was in the act of offering up the only descendant he would ever see. Abraham had learned to fully rely on the promise of God.

Selected Readings:
- **Hebrews 11:17-19** for Abraham's faith in the potential sacrifice of Isaac.
- **John 1:29** for John the Baptist's announcement of Jesus as the Lamb of God.

Facts to Know

Rebekah	wife of Isaac
Laban	Rebekah's brother
Nahor	Abraham's brother
burnt offering	an animal burned as a sacrifice to God

Memory Verse

Genesis 22:7-8
And Isaac spake unto Abraham his father and said, Behold the fire and the wood: but where is the lamb? And Abraham said, My son, God will provide himself a lamb for a burnt offering.

1. What great act of sacrifice was Abraham willing to perform for God?
   Abraham was willing to sacrifice his own son.

2. Abraham told Isaac that God would provide a lamb for the sacrifice. What lamb did God provide?
   God provided a lamb in the thicket for the sacrifice, as a substitute for Isaac.

3. What did John the Baptist call Jesus in John 1:29?
   John said, "Behold the Lamb of God who takes away the sins of the world."

26

Teacher Note

Spiritual lesson: No matter how dark and despairing your situation, trust in the Lord, He will provide.

BOOKS OF THE OLD TESTAMENT. See Instructions in Teacher Guidelines.
Teach:

• **Genesis**	**Book of Beginnings**
• **Exodus**	**Deliverance from Egyptian Bondage**
• **Leviticus**	**Book of the Law**
• **Numbers**	**Wilderness Wanderings**
• **Deuteronomy**	**Second Book of the Law**

A Wife for Isaac   Genesis 22-24

Comprehension Questions

1. How did God reward Abraham for his faithfulness?
   God gave Abraham so many offspring that he became the father of many nations.

2. What did Abraham ask his servant to do for him?
   Abraham asked his servant to go to Haran, where Abraham had come from and where
   his relatives still lived, to choose a wife for Isaac. (p. 42)

3. Where specifically did Abraham's servant go to find a wife for Isaac?
   His servant went to Mesopotamia, to the city of Nahor, in Haran. (p. 43)

4. How was the servant to know whom God intended for Isaac?
   When the servant said, "Let down your pitcher, so that I may drink," Isaac's intended
   would say, "Drink! And I will give your camels a drink also." (p. 44)

5. Find on Unit 1 Map A: ☐ Mesopotamia

   ☐ Tigris River   ☐ Euphrates River   ☐ Haran (Nahor)

   27

Activities

pp. 42-43   Identify Abraham and his servant. What is Abraham asking the servant to do? How many
              camels did the servant take?
              Abraham is asking his servant to go back to their homeland and seek a wife for Isaac. The
              servant packed ten camels.

pp. 44-45   How did people obtain water for their needs? Describe what is happening.
              Women went to the community well and drew up water and filled their pitchers or jars.
              Abraham's servant meets Rebekah, who gives him a drink and also water for his camels.

p. 46   What is Rebekah holding? What is she telling her mother?
              Rebekah is holding the gold bracelet that Abraham's servant gave her. Rebekah is telling her
              mother about the stranger she met at the well who is the servant of her father's relatives.

p. 47   Who are meeting for the first time in this picture?
              Rebekah descends from her camel, veils her face, and comes to meet her future husband, Isaac.

Lesson 7

Background and Summary

After the earnest prayers of Isaac (Gen. 25:21), the womb of Rebekah is opened and she gives birth to two sons. These sons, however, are born struggling with one another (Gen. 25:22-23). In this struggle they will remain for most of their days. Through the struggle of Esau and Jacob, we will see that God's blessing follows an unlikely route. Though Esau was the firstborn, Jacob will actually receive the blessing. Jacob is the son of God's choosing. The struggle between these two brothers comes to a head when Jacob, with his mother's help, deceives his father and effectively robs Esau of his blessing as the firstborn.

As Jacob flees the wrath of his brother, he rests in Bethel and experiences a fantastic vision in a dream from the Lord. God shows him a ladder upon which angels ascend and descend. This image alludes to the project in Babel: a tower that could reach Heaven (Gen. 11). The significance of this allusion, however, demonstrates the reverse of Babel's project: God, not man, is making a way between Heaven and mankind. God will make a way through the seed of Jacob (Gen. 28:13-15). Like his father and grandfather, Jacob receives God's blessing and responds by making a vow of faithfulness to God (Gen. 28:20-21). The faithful will rely on God's promise.

What can we learn from the mistake Esau made? He gave up his birthright because he allowed his carnal desires to overrule his better judgment (*carnal* comes from a Latin word that means "flesh"). How foolish to listen to your stomach more than your good sense!

The spiritual lesson here teaches us that we cannot be controlled by our bodies or our appetites, or we will lose out on the best that God has in store for us. In this way, our minds must be filled with thoughts of God's heavenly ways and not man's sinful or fleshly practices. Consider Paul's instruction about this in Philippians 4:8.

Lesson 7 (pp. 48-55)   Esau and Jacob

Facts to Know

Jacob	Isaac's son; received his father's blessing
Esau	Isaac's son; sold his birthright to Jacob
Jacob's Ladder	Jacob's dream, in which angels were ascending and descending a ladder to Heaven
"He sold his birthright for a mess of pottage."	to sell your future for immediate pleasure
birthright	family inheritance for the firstborn

Memory Verse

Genesis 25:27

Esau was a cunning hunter, a man of the field; and Jacob was a plain man dwelling in tents.

1. Contrast the appearance and activities of Jacob and Esau.
   Esau had red hair all over and was a hunter, an outdoors man. Jacob was a plain man, dwelling in tents. (p. 48)
2. Which of the two twins was favored by the father Isaac? Why?
   Esau was Isaac's favorite; Isaac loved to eat the meat Esau hunted.
3. Which of the two twins was favored by the mother Rebekah? Why?
   Jacob was Rebekah's favorite; Jacob dwelled at home in the tents.
4. Which twin was the oldest and possessed the inheritance by birthright?
   Esau was the natural heir because he was the firstborn.

28

Vocabulary and Expressions

1. **score**: twenty
2. **venison**: deer meat
3. **birthright**: family inheritance for the firstborn
4. **quiver**: holder for arrows
5. **slay**: to kill
6. **yoke**: harness for a beast of burden
7. **savory**: salty or flavorful
8. **fetch**: to get or bring
9. **kids**: young goats
10. **revenged**: settled a score; got a payback
11. **fury**: rage or anger
12. **firstborn**: heir of blessing
13. **curse**: punishment; opposite of blessing
14. **deceiver**: one who hides the truth or one who lies
15. **mourn**: to grieve for a loss

Jacob's Flight   Genesis 25-28

Comprehension Questions

1. What is a score? What is three score? How old was Isaac when Rebekah bore him twins?
   A score is twenty; three score is sixty; Isaac was three score or sixty years old when his twins were born. (p. 48)

2. Why did Esau sell his birthright? What does this say about him?
   Esau sold his future inheritance for something to eat immediately. He lived for the present rather than planning for the future. (pp. 48-49)

3. What did Jacob and Rebekah do to deceive Isaac?
   Jacob appeared to Isaac wearing goat fur and Esau's robe, so he would look and smell like Esau and then tricked Isaac into giving Jacob the blessing that belonged to Esau. (pp. 50-51)

4. What was the blessing Isaac gave Jacob? Esau?
   Isaac's blessing to Jacob was that nations would bow down to him, people would serve him, everyone who cursed him would be cursed, and everyone who blessed him would be blessed. Isaac's blessing to Esau was that he should serve his brother, Jacob, but it would come to pass that he would acquire power and break this bond to Jacob.

5. Why did Jacob flee and what dream did he have when he stopped for sleep?
   Jacob fled because he was afraid of Esau's anger. When he stopped for rest, he dreamed of a ladder reaching to Heaven with angels ascending and descending.

6. What did God tell Jacob during his dream?
   God told Jacob that the land upon which he lay was to be his and his children's. He also told him that He would guard him everywhere he went and would not leave him. (p. 54)

7. Where did Jacob place a pillar to mark the land that God had promised him?
   Bethel (p. 55)

8. Find on Unit 1 Map A: ☐ Haran
   on Unit 2 Map: ☐ Beersheba ☐ Bethel ☐ Shechem

29

BOOKS OF OLD TESTAMENT
Teach book "subtitles" listed in Teacher Guidelines.

Review:
   • **Genesis**
   • **Exodus**
   • **Leviticus**
   • **Numbers**
   • **Deuteronomy**
Teach:
   • **Joshua**
   • **Judges**
   • **Ruth**

Teacher Notes

On page 55, Jacob makes his faithful vow to God and says, "This stone which I have set up for a pillar will be God's house, and of all that you give to me, O God, I will give a tenth to you."
What is this offering called today?
a tithe

Activities

pp. 48-49   Identify the two men. Explain what is happening.
Esau has come in from hunting and is famished. He looks red and has his quiver and arrows. Jacob is asking for the birthright in return for the soup he has cooked.

p. 50   Identify the two people. Explain what is happening.
Jacob has brought two kids so Rebekah can make skins for him to wear and deceive Isaac.

p. 51   Identify the three people and what is happening.
Jacob is wearing the skins, and Isaac is giving the blessing as Rebekah looks on.

pp. 54-55   Who is sleeping? What is the dream?
Jacob is sleeping, and his dream is called Jacob's Ladder.

Memory Verse Review: #19 in Appendix. Give the first word or two of a verse and see how many students can complete it.

Lesson 8

Background and Summary

Jacob's flight from his brother takes him to the land of his maternal uncle, Laban. After twenty years, God greatly blesses Jacob by giving him many sons through Rachel, Leah, and their concubines. Thus, Jacob's prolonged stay in Haran, which Laban orchestrated by deception and greed, God has used to fulfill his promise of descendants (Gen. 30:27).

As Jacob flees from the home of his father-in-law, he has to face his brother. The memory of how he wronged his brother haunts the mind of Jacob as he makes his way back home (Gen. 32:7). In the night, Jacob wrestles with a divine envoy and is crippled by the angel. When the struggle persists, Jacob demands a blessing, but the angel demands a confession: "What is your name?" Weakened by the experience, Jacob owns up to his past. He is Jacob, "the deceiver, the heel grabber," but God renames and blesses him as Israel, "God's fighter" (Gen. 32:24-32 and again in 35:10-12). In this humbled state, he encounters his brother and bows low before him. Amazed by the mercy of Esau, Jacob gives a gift to his brother because he has seen the face of God and has received His grace (Gen. 33:10-11).

Selected Reading:
Psalm 46:1-7 for a beautiful song of praise to the God of Jacob.

Relate the psalmist's praise of God as a refuge to the way God has been Jacob's strength in this lesson.

Lesson 8 (pp. 56-63)   Jacob and Rachel

Facts to Know

Laban	Rebekah's brother; father of Leah and Rachel
Rachel	Jacob's beautiful wife
Leah	Jacob's plain wife
Joseph	beloved son of Jacob and Rachel
Israel	Jacob's new name, given for contending with God

Memory Verse

Genesis 29:20

Jacob served seven years for Rachel and they seemed but a few days, for the love he had for her.

1. How did Jacob serve for Rachel?
   Jacob worked for Laban, raising sheep.

2. How long did Jacob serve Laban for Rachel, and why?
   Jacob agreed to work seven years as payment for Rachel because he loved her, but ended up working fourteen years because Laban tricked him.

3. Explain why "seven years seemed but a few days."
   Jacob loved Rachel so much, the reward would exceed the price.

30

Vocabulary and Expressions

1. **chide**: to scold; to reprimand
2. **brethren**: members of a religion or tribe (archaic plural of *brother*)
3. **drove**: a herd of livestock driven together
4. **appease**: to pacify by giving in to demands

Jacob and Rachel   Genesis 29-33

Comprehension Questions

1. Where did Jacob go after he stole his brother's birthright? What is the significance of this location?

   Jacob fled to Haran, the home of Abraham before he came into Canaan, and the location where Abraham sent the servant to find a wife for Isaac (Rebekah).

2. What agreement did Laban and Jacob make regarding Rachel?

   Jacob would work for Laban for seven years if at the end of that time Laban would give Jacob his youngest daughter, Rachel. (p. 57)

3. How did Laban deceive Jacob?

   Laban brought Leah, his eldest daughter, to Jacob instead of Rachel. (p. 58)

4. Which of Jacob's wives had many sons? Which wife was barren until God opened her womb?

   Leah had many sons. Rachel had two, Joseph and Benjamin, after God opened her womb.

5. Why did God give Jacob a new name? What does it mean to "wrestle with an angel"?

   God said, "Your name shall no longer be called Jacob but Israel, for you have contended with God and prevailed." Israel means "he who struggles with God." To "wrestle with an angel" means to fight and overcome man's desires for himself and submit to God's will. (p. 61)

6. How did Esau treat Jacob when the brothers were reunited?

   Esau ran to meet Jacob, embraced him, fell on his neck and kissed him, and they wept together. (p. 62)

7. Find on Unit 1 Map A: ☐ Haran
   on Unit 2 Map: ☐ Beersheba ☐ Bethel ☐ Shechem ☐ Hebron

31

BOOKS OF OLD TESTAMENT
Teach book "subtitles" listed in Teacher Guidelines.

Review:
- **Genesis**
- **Exodus**
- **Leviticus**
- **Numbers**
- **Deuteronomy**
- **Joshua**
- **Judges**
- **Ruth**

Teach:
- **I & II Samuel**
- **I & II Kings**
- **I & II Chronicles**

Activities

pp. 56-57   Who are the two people in the top picture? The three people in the bottom?
   Jacob and Rachel have just met. Jacob has opened the well for Rachel's flock to drink. In the bottom picture, Jacob and Laban are meeting while beautiful Rachel looks on.

pp. 58-59   Identify Laban, Rachel, and Jacob. What is happening? Why is Rachel sitting?
   Jacob is watching as Laban goes through his belongings. Rachel is sitting on her camel saddle, where she has hidden the family images so Laban will not find them.

p. 61   What is Jacob doing?
   Jacob is wrestling with an angel all night. God changes his name to Israel after this. This is the night before he meets Esau again.

pp. 62-63   Identify Jacob and Esau. Who is kneeling? Why? What is happening in the bottom picture?
   Jacob and Rachel are kneeling to Esau. Jacob had not seen Esau for 20 years, since he had stolen Esau's birthright. In the bottom picture, Jacob is offering him the flocks and cattle as a gift to amend for stealing his birthright.

Lesson 9

Background and Summary

From very early in the account of Joseph's life, we see the blessing of God rest on him through the love of his father, Israel. At this point, the blessing of God manifests itself in the form of Joseph's ability to interpret dreams. This special ability, however, is not well received by his older brothers, another example of God's blessing landing on a recipient unforeseen by men. Joseph's brothers envy him so much that they want to kill him. They avoid murder in view of an opportunity to make some money (Gen. 37:18-36). Though Jacob is crushed by the falsified news that his favorite son is dead, God planned this turn of events for a future good.

While in Egypt, God's blessing continues to follow Joseph into Potiphar's house and into the Egyptian jailhouse (Gen. 39:1-5, 21-23). Everything Joseph touches in Egypt is made to prosper, and he interprets more dreams with increasingly important clients.

Though he receives horrible mistreatment from his own family, Joseph continues to trust and hope in the God of his fathers.

Selected Reading:
   Acts 7:9-10 for Stephen's words about God's faithfulness to Joseph.

Facts to Know

Joseph	Jacob's favorite son by Rachel
coat of many colors	Jacob's gift to his favorite son, Joseph
Reuben	Joseph's oldest brother, who saved him from death
Pharaoh	King of Egypt
Potiphar	officer of Pharaoh who bought Joseph
famine	lack of food due to crop failure
butler and baker	Pharaoh's servants in prison whose dreams Joseph interpreted

Memory Verse

   Genesis 40:8

   And Joseph said, "Do not interpretations belong to God?"

1. What was the butler's dream?
   The butler saw a vine with three branches that budded and produced grapes. He was holding Pharaoh's cup. He pressed the grapes into the cup and gave it to Pharaoh.

2. What was Joseph's interpretation?
   Within three days, Pharaoh would restore the butler to his place in his household.

3. What was the baker's dream?
   He had three baskets of bread on his head. The top basket held baked goods, which were being eaten by birds.

4. What was Joseph's interpretation?
   Within three days, Pharaoh would hang him and birds would eat his flesh.

32

Vocabulary and Expressions

1. **dwelt**: lived
2. **sheaf, sheaves**: bundle(s) of wheat
3. **binding sheaves**: gathering the harvest
4. **caravan**: convoy or procession of travelers
5. **sackcloth**: mourning garment
6. **overseer**: boss or manager
7. **dungeon**: underground prison
8. **butler**: male house servant

Joseph in Egypt   Genesis 37-40

Comprehension Questions

1. Describe Joseph's two dreams concerning his brothers.

   First, Joseph's sheaves stood upright while those of the brothers bowed over to his sheaf. Second, the sun, moon, and stars bowed down to Joseph. (p. 64)

2. Why did Joseph's brothers plot against him?

   They were envious because Joseph was his father's favorite and because they feared his dreams would be true, that he would rule over them. (p. 65)

3. What was Reuben's plan to save Joseph, and how was it foiled?

   After convincing his brothers to throw Joseph into the pit alive, Reuben planned to return and take him out, but the brothers had sold him to a caravan of traders. (p. 65)

4. Who bought Joseph as a slave in Egypt and how did he prosper?

   Potiphar bought him and made him head over his whole household.

5. Why was Joseph put in prison? How did he prosper there? What does this tell you about Joseph?

   The wife of Potiphar lied about Joseph mocking her. Joseph was put in charge of the prison. Joseph was a smart, trustworthy leader. Joseph succeeded in every situation because God was with him. (p. 68)

6. What did Joseph ask of the butler?

   To remember him, mention him to Pharaoh, and help him get out of prison. (p. 70)

7. Did the butler do what Joseph asked?

   No, the butler forgot Joseph. (p. 70)

8. Find on 1) globe or world map and/or 2) Unit 2 Map: ☐ Africa ☐ Egypt ☐ Nile River and Delta ☐ Mediterranean Sea ☐ Red Sea ☐ Persian Gulf ☐ Arabia ☐ Sinai Peninsula ☐ Canaan

33

BOOKS OF OLD TESTAMENT
Teach book "subtitles" listed in Teacher Guidelines.

Review:
- **Genesis**
- **Exodus**
- **Leviticus**
- **Numbers**
- **Deuteronomy**
- **Joshua**
- **Judges**
- **Ruth**
- **I & II Samuel**
- **I & II Kings**
- **I & II Chronicles**

Teach:
- **Ezra**
- **Nehemiah**
- **Esther**

Activities

pp. 64-65   Identify the two people.
Jacob gives Joseph, his favorite son, a coat of colors.

p. 66   What are the brothers telling Jacob? What is Jacob holding?
The brothers are telling Jacob that Joseph is dead. Jacob holds Joseph's coat, stained with blood.

p. 67   Who is traveling the journey depicted on the map? Where is the caravan going? What is the name of the tribe in the caravan? Who are they descended from?
Joseph is in the caravan of Ishmaelites, the descendants of Ishmael, son of Hagar. The caravan is traveling to Egypt.

pp. 68-69   What is happening? Who is the Egyptian on the steps?
Potiphar, the Egyptian, is buying Joseph as a slave from the Ishmaelites.

p. 69   Who are these two men, and what are they doing?
This is the butler's dream in which he squeezes grapes into the royal cup of wine for Pharaoh.

p. 70   Explain the picture at the bottom of the page.
This is the baker's dream in which birds eat from the top of three baskets on his head.

Memory Verse Review: #20-21 in Appendix. Give the first word or two of a verse and see how many students can complete it.

Lesson 10

Background and Summary

By interpreting the dreams of the Pharaoh in Egypt and overseeing the famine relief efforts, Joseph, by God's design, arises to a place of prominence and blessing in that kingdom. His status in Egypt provides him the means and the opportunity to greatly aid his brothers when they are driven to Egypt because of the famine in Canaan.

When Joseph's brothers arrive, he does not reveal himself to them. Instead, he orchestrates a plan to humble his brothers and remind them of what they had done to him years ago. He keeps Simeon in Egypt until they bring Benjamin back to him. In fear, the brothers return to their father.

Facts to Know

Ephraim and Manasseh	Joseph's sons born in Egypt
Benjamin	Joseph's youngest brother; Rachel's second son
Simeon	Joseph's brother who was kept behind in Egypt
kine	cattle

Memory Verse

Genesis 41:26

The seven good kine are seven years; and the seven good ears are seven years; the dream is one.

1. Describe the two dreams of the Pharaoh.
   First, seven fat cows were devoured by seven scrawny cows, which remained scrawny. Second, seven full ears of corn were devoured by seven thin and withered ears. (p. 71)

2. How did Joseph interpret the dreams?
   There will be seven years of great plenty throughout the whole land of Egypt, and after that there will come seven years of famine. The famine years will eat up all of the grain of the years of plenty, just as the skinny cows ate the fat ones and still remained skinny. (p. 72)

3. What did Joseph tell Pharaoh about his power to interpret dreams?
   Only God has the power to interpret dreams, so when Joseph tells the meaning of a dream, it is God speaking through him.

4. Why does Joseph say Pharaoh's two dreams are one?
   The meaning of both dreams is the same.

34

Vocabulary and Expressions

1. **discreet**: showing prudence and wise self-restraint in speech and behavior
2. **famished**: weak from hunger
3. **linen**: light fabric for warm climates
4. **interpretation**: reading or explanation
5. **ear of corn**: single corn on the cob

Joseph's Brothers in Egypt   Genesis 41-43

Comprehension Questions

1. What did Joseph recommend to the Pharaoh?

   Joseph recommended that Pharaoh appoint a wise and discreet governor, who should gather a fifth of the harvest in the good years and store it secretly in the cities to draw on during the seven years of famine. (pp. 72-73)

2. How did Pharaoh reward Joseph for his assistance?

   Pharaoh chose Joseph to be his governor. He put him in charge of the royal household and civil management of the kingdom. (p. 73)

3. What did Joseph do to his brothers when they arrived and asked him for food?

   He pretended not to know them and accused them of being spies. (p. 76)

4. Who did Joseph tell the brothers to bring back to prove they were not spies? Why do you think he did this?

   Joseph asked to see the youngest brother, Benjamin, who had stayed behind. He wanted to test his brothers to see if they had changed, or if they would sacrifice Benjamin as they had sacrificed him. (p. 76)

5. What did the brothers find in their grain sacks on the way home? Why were they so afraid?

   They found the money they had paid for the grain. They were afraid they would be accused of stealing the money and confirmed as spies.

6. Why did Jacob love Benjamin and Joseph more than his other sons?

   Benjamin and Joseph were the sons of his favorite wife, Rachel.

7. Find on 1) globe or world map and 2) Unit 2 Map: ☐ Africa ☐ Egypt

   ☐ Nile River and Delta ☐ Mediterranean Sea ☐ Red Sea

   ☐ Persian Gulf ☐ Arabia ☐ Sinai Peninsula ☐ Canaan

   35

BOOKS OF OLD TESTAMENT
Teach book "subtitles" listed in Teacher Guidelines.

Review:
- **Genesis**
- **Exodus**
- **Leviticus**
- **Numbers**
- **Deuteronomy**
- **Joshua**
- **Judges**
- **Ruth**
- **I & II Samuel**
- **I & II Kings**
- **I & II Chronicles**
- **Ezra**
- **Nehemiah**
- **Esther**

Activities

pp. 70-71   Explain the picture at the top of the page.
The seven thin cows are coming out of the river to eat the seven fat cows in Pharaoh's dream.

p. 72   Identify Pharaoh and Joseph. What is Pharaoh giving Joseph? Why?
Pharaoh is giving Joseph a ring that makes him ruler of the land of Egypt.

p. 73   Explain what is happening. Joseph is riding in the second royal chariot, and the people are bowing before him because he is now the ruler of Egypt.

p. 75   Describe what is happening in the picture. Joseph's brothers have come to ask for food and they are bowing before him, just as the dream predicted many years before.

p. 76   Why is Joseph weeping? Joseph overhears Reuben saying his brothers were accused of being spies as punishment for throwing Joseph into a pit many years ago.

p. 77   Explain what is happening. The brothers discover the money they had paid for the grain in their grain sacks on the way home.

p. 78   Identify Jacob and Benjamin. Where is Benjamin going? Why?
Jacob is embracing Benjamin before he makes the trip to Egypt to obtain more grain.

Review Lesson: Unit 2

Instructions

Use this Review Lesson to support mastery of the material presented in the previous five lessons. Drill the Facts to Know orally or have a Facts to Know Bee. Places to Know should be identified on the maps in this lesson. Events to Know will be reviewed in the timeline exercise which follows. Students may work independently on these two pages of the Review, but answers should be checked in class. A test for this unit is included in the back of this book.

Events to Know in Salvation History

The Patriarchs cont.
God Provides a Lamb
A Wife for Isaac
Twins Born to Struggle
A Birthright Stolen
The Flight to Haran
A Stairway to Heaven
Labor of Love
Jacob's New Name
Twelve Sons
Coat of Many Colors
Joseph the Dreamer
Dreamer Becomes a Slave
Dreams in Prison
Pharaoh's Dreams
Pharaoh's Right-Hand Man
A Famine in Egypt

People to Know
Isaac and Rebekah
Jacob and Esau
Israel
Rachel and Leah
Laban
Reuban, Simeon, Levi,
    Judah
Joseph
Benjamin
Potiphar
Butler and Baker
Pharaoh
Ephraim and Manasseh

The Three Patriarchs
Abraham
Isaac
Jacob

The Three Patriarch Wives
Sarah
Rebekah
Rachel

Places to Know
Canaan
Egypt
Sinai Peninsula
Bethel
Beersheba
Hebron
Shechem
Nile River and Delta
Mediterranean Sea
Red Sea

Words to Know
score: twenty
burnt offering: an animal burned as a sacrifice to God
famine: a lack of food due to crop failure
kine: cattle
birthright: family inheritance for the firstborn son
firstborn: heir of blessing; first son
venison: deer meat
butler: male servant in household
sackcloth: mourning garment
savory: salty or flavorful
sheaf, sheaves: bundle(s) of wheat

Books of the O.T.
Genesis
Exodus
Leviticus
Numbers
Deuteronomy
Joshua
Judges
Ruth
I II Samuel
I II Kings
I II Chronicles
Ezra
Nehemiah
Esther

36

Review Lesson: Unit 2 (Lessons 6-10)

Give the corresponding word or phrase:

1. The king of Egypt _____ Pharaoh
2. The three patriarchs _____ Abraham, Isaac, Jacob
3. The two sons of Jacob and Rachel _____ Joseph and Benjamin
4. Jacob's two wives _____ Leah and Rachel
5. Jacob's name was changed to _____ Israel
6. Isaac's twin sons _____ Jacob and Esau
7. Pharaoh's servants, in prison with Joseph __ butler and baker
8. She lied about Joseph _____ Potiphar's wife
9. Jacob's beautiful wife _____ Rachel
10. Egyptian who bought Joseph _____ Potiphar
11. Joseph's youngest brother _____ Benjamin
12. Joseph's two dreams _____ brothers' sheaves bowed to his sheaf;
    _____ sun, moon, and stars bowed down to him
13. The three patriarch wives _____ Sarah, Rebekah, Rachel
14. Jacob's favorite son _____ Joseph
15. Jacob's dream _____ ladder with angels
16. He had a coat of many colors _____ Joseph
17. Joseph's two sons _____ Ephraim and Manasseh
18. The number of years of plenty and famine _ seven
19. Jacob's plain wife _____ Leah
20. Pharaoh's two dreams _____ lean and fat cows; blasted and fat ears
21. He sold his birthright for a mess of pottage Esau

Match up the Words to Know:

K	score	A. first son; heir of blessing
E	burnt offering	B. male servant
G	famine	C. deer meat
F	kine	D. salty or flavorful
J	birthright	E. an animal burned as a sacrifice to God
A	firstborn	F. cattle
C	venison	G. a lack of food due to crop failure
B	butler	H. garment worn for mourning
H	sackcloth	I. a bundle of wheat
D	savory	J. family inheritance for the firstborn son
I	sheaf	K. twenty

37

Review Lesson: Unit 2

Old Testament Drill Questions

All of the short answer review questions from each Review Lesson have been compiled in Appendix 2. Continue to review them throughout the year. They are great for bees and competitions.

Review Lesson: Unit 2

Timeline Review

Elementary-age children do not have a well-developed sense of time, especially time long ago and time over a long period. Putting events and people in order is also an advanced skill. These timelines are designed to teach beginning skills in creating a mental timeline of history. Students cannot do this work independently; this is a teacher-directed learning activity. Begin by looking at "The Age of the Patriarchs: Jacob and Esau" and putting them in order; then add them to the timeline. Next, go to "The Age of the Patriarchs: Joseph and his Brothers" and do the same. Lastly, help students add names from People to Know to match the events.

Salvation History Timeline

The events of Salvation History are out of order! Number them in correct order (1-16). Then match people from the Review Lesson with events. Some people may be used more than once and in different combinations than shown in the list.

The Age of the Patriarchs:
Jacob and Esau

- _9_ Jacob's New Name
- _8_ Twelve Sons
- _2_ A Wife for Isaac
- _6_ A Stairway to Heaven
- _3_ Twins Born to Struggle
- _4_ A Birthright Stolen
- _7_ Labor of Love
- _5_ The Flight to Haran
- _1_ God Provides a Lamb

The Age of the Patriarchs:
Joseph and His Brothers

- _12_ Dreamer Becomes a Slave
- _10_ A Coat of Many Colors
- _16_ A Famine in Egypt
- _15_ Pharaoh's Right-Hand Man
- _11_ Joseph, the Dreamer
- _14_ Pharaoh's Dreams
- _13_ Dreams in Prison

Events	Period	People
	Patriarchs	
God Provides a Lamb		Isaac
A Wife for Isaac		Rebekah
Twins Born to Struggle		Jacob and Esau
A Birthright Stolen		Jacob and Esau, Isaac and Rebekah
The Flight to Haran		Jacob, Laban
A Stairway to Heaven		Jacob
Labor of Love		Laban, Leah, Rachel, Jacob
Twelve Sons		Rachel and Leah
Jacob's New Name		Jacob to Israel
A Coat of Many Colors		Joseph
Joseph, the Dreamer		Joseph, the 11 brothers
Dreamer Becomes a Slave		Reuben, Potiphar
Dreams in Prison		Joseph, cup-bearer, baker
Pharaoh's Dreams		Pharaoh, Joseph
Pharaoh's Right-Hand Man		Joseph and Pharaoh
Famine in Egypt		Joseph, Benjamin, Simeon

38

Review Lesson: Unit 2 (Lessons 6-10)

Scripture Memorization

Check each box if you can recite the Scripture verse from memory. Write each from memory or teacher dictation. Be accurate.

☐ **Genesis 22:7-8** _____

And Isaac spake unto Abraham his father and said, Behold the fire and the wood: but

where is the lamb? And Abraham said, My son, God will provide himself a lamb for a

burnt offering.

☐ **Genesis 25:27** Esau was a cunning hunter, a man of the field; and Jacob was a

plain man dwelling in tents.

☐ **Genesis 29:20** Jacob served seven years for Rachel and they seemed but a few

days, for the love he had for her.

☐ **Genesis 40:8** And Joseph said, "Do not interpretations belong to God?"

☐ **Genesis 41:26** The seven good kine are seven years; and the seven good ears

are seven years; the dream is one.

Write the Books of History:

1. _____ Joshua
2. _____ Judges
3. _____ Ruth
4. _____ I Samuel
5. _____ II Samuel
6. _____ I Kings
7. _____ II Kings
8. _____ I Chronicles
9. _____ II Chronicles
10. _____ Ezra
11. _____ Nehemiah
12. _____ Esther

Write the Books of the Law:

1. _____ Genesis
2. _____ Exodus
3. _____ Leviticus
4. _____ Numbers
5. _____ Deuteronomy

39

Review Lesson: Unit 2

Memory Verses

To recite memory verses, give the first few words and let students complete the verse orally. Students may write the verse from memory, from dictation, or copy it.

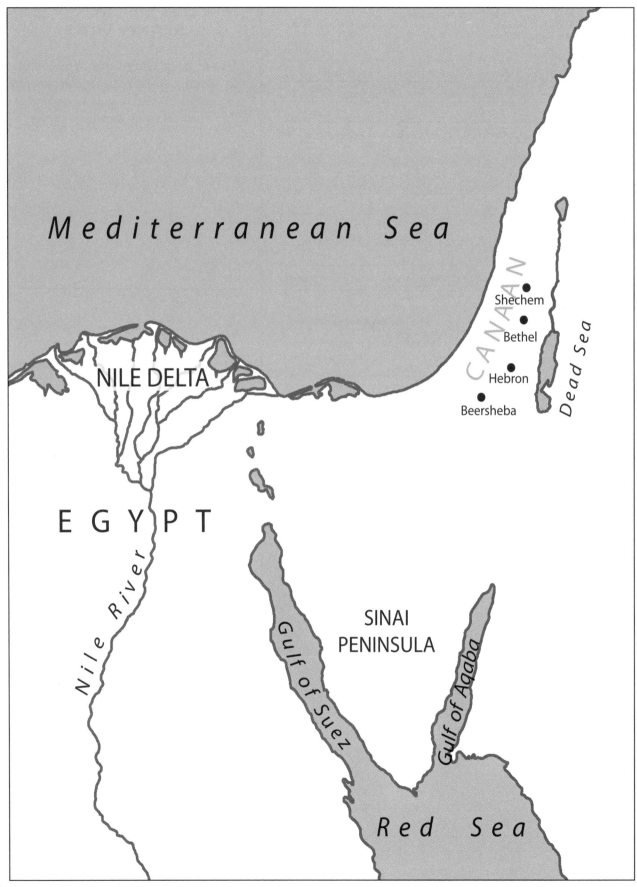

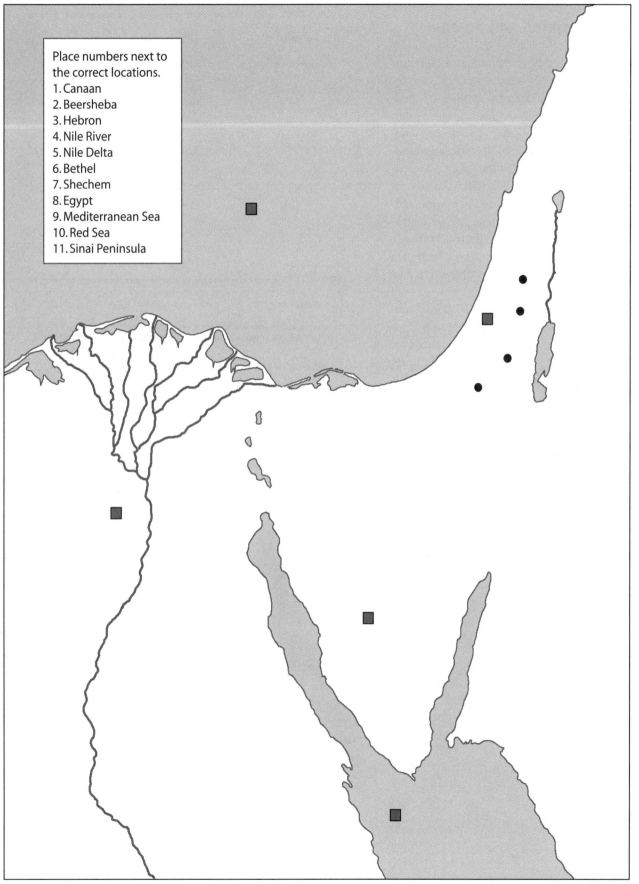

Place numbers next to
the correct locations.
1. Canaan
2. Beersheba
3. Hebron
4. Nile River
5. Nile Delta
6. Bethel
7. Shechem
8. Egypt
9. Mediterranean Sea
10. Red Sea
11. Sinai Peninsula

Lesson 11

Background and Summary

When the brothers return with Benjamin, Joseph can barely keep his composure to hide his identity from his brothers. When Joseph orders them to return to Canaan without Benjamin, Judah, the brother who engineered the sale of Joseph, arises to offer himself instead of the youngest (Gen. 44:18). Joseph sees that Judah knows of their father's sufferings due to his sin, and Joseph has compassion on his brothers. Then Joseph reveals himself to his brothers, forgives them, and explains how God has brought good out of their terrible sins (Gen. 45:1-15).

In this way, the story of Joseph again emphasizes the truth that no matter what we think of the difficult circumstances in life, God is in control of it all. Working everything out for the good of those who love Him, God remains faithful to His promises and steadfast in His love for His people. We can take a lesson from Joseph's ability to trust God in difficult times and ultimately see God's good hand at work in all things.

Selected Reading:
Romans 8:28 for God's promise of providential protection for His people.

Facts to Know

Hebrews	the children of Israel
Egyptians	people from Egypt; where Joseph ruled
Goshen	fertile territory in Egypt, east of the Nile delta; granted by Pharaoh to Joseph and his descendants

Memory Verse

Genesis 45:4,5,8

I am Joseph your brother, whom ye sold into Egypt. Now therefore be not grieved with yourselves, for it was not you that sent me hither, but God.

1. What is the first thing Joseph asked his brothers after revealing his identity?
   Joseph asked, "Is my father still alive?"

2. What does "be not grieved with yourselves" mean?
   Do not be angry with yourselves.

3. What does "sent me hither" mean?
   Sent me here (to Egypt)

42

Vocabulary and Expressions

1. **balm**: medicinal oil from tree
2. **myrrh**: tree resin used as incense and perfume
3. **hither**: *archaic adverb for* here
4. **yearn**: to long for; to want

Joseph Reveals Who He Is   Genesis 43-45

Comprehension Questions

1. Why were Joseph's brothers afraid when they were invited into his house?

   They were afraid they would be accused of stealing the money that had mysteriously appeared in their grain sacks. (p. 80)

2. Describe the seating arrangement at supper.

   The brothers sat before Joseph in order from the firstborn to the youngest. The Egyptians ate separately, because it was against their law to dine with Hebrews. (p. 81)

3. What did Joseph do to test his brothers to see if they had truly changed?

   He planted his silver cup in Benjamin's sack and sent his steward to overtake the brothers and bring them back, demanding that Benjamin be his slave for this theft. (p. 82)

4. How did the brothers redeem themselves? Who offered to be a slave in Benjamin's place? How was this the opposite of what they had done to Joseph?

   Judah said they would all remain as slaves and when Joseph declined such a harsh punishment, Judah asked if he could take Benjamin's place. The brothers offered to sacrifice themselves for Benjamin, which was the opposite of how they had treated Joseph when they sold him into slavery.

5. Why did Joseph forgive his brothers for their mistreatment of him?

   They had redeemed themselves by their willingness to sacrifice themselves for Benjamin. Joseph further said that God had acted in order to send him ahead and arrange the grain storage that would save their lives during the famine. God had brought good out of their evil deeds. (p. 85)

6. How did Joseph rescue his father and his brothers?

   With five years of famine left, Joseph arranged for his family to live in the land of Goshen where they could survive. (p. 85)

43

Activities

Patriarch Family Tree

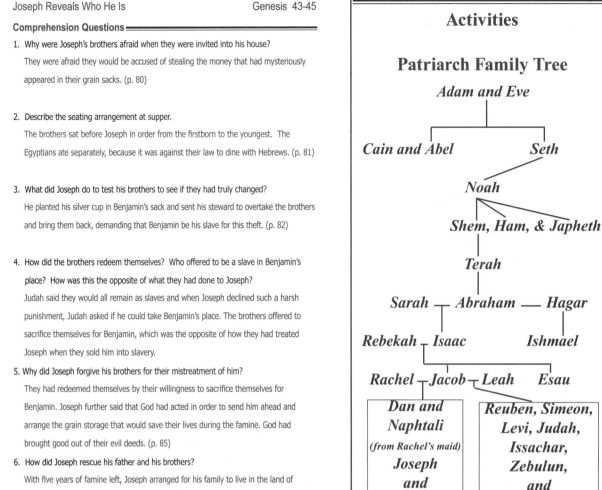

Draw a family tree as shown above.

pp. 79-85   Find Benjamin in each picture on these pages.

p. 79   What is Benjamin doing?
             Benjamin is meeting Joseph.

pp. 80-81   What is happening?
             The brothers are eating the feast Joseph has prepared for them.

p. 82   What has happened?
             Pharaoh's stewards have found Joseph's cup in Benjamin's sack.

p. 83   Who is pleading with Joseph? Why?
             Judah is pleading with Joseph to save Benjamin's life. He offers himself in Benjamin's place.

p. 84   Count the brothers in the picture. Are they all there?
             Yes, all 12 sons of Jacob are there.

Draw a family tree as shown above.
Ask students **who begat whom** and draw this family tree chart on the blackboard. If you make a worksheet with pre-drawn lines, students will be able to reproduce this chart on their worksheets as you draw it.

Lesson 12

Background and Summary

The genealogical account of Genesis concludes with the news that Jacob and his sons have settled in Egypt in order to survive the effects of famine at home in Canaan. The Lord comforts Jacob in leaving the Promised Land for Egypt by promising that He will surely bring them back. For now, the family line survives by staying in Egypt. Recognizing God's care for his family, Jacob pronounces a blessing on Pharaoh (Gen. 47:7-10). The old, frail, refugee father of seventy descendants blesses the king of the wealthiest and greatest empire in the Ancient Near Eastern world! Here, the significance is not the one who blesses (Jacob), but the source of the blessing (the God of Jacob).

Pharaoh receives the blessing and honors the budding Israelite family with the choicest land of Egypt: Goshen (Gen. 47:11). As Jacob sees his death approaching, he calls his sons together to pronounce blessings on them (Gen. 49). What started as a sparse line of sons and grandsons will grow into a great nation of people divided into tribes headed by the twelve sons of Jacob, of which Judah will rule (Gen. 49:8-12). The significance of Judah's family becomes plain in the genealogy of Matthew 1; David, Solomon, Josiah, and Jesus are descendants! Solely by God's provision, the promised seed finally begins to flourish and, in time, will regain the land of promise, carrying the bones of Joseph with them.

The Nile River empties into the Mediterranean Sea and flows north, not south as we are used to.

Selected Readings:
- **Hebrews 11:21-22** for the faith of Jacob and Joseph that their descendants would return to the Promised Land from Egypt.
- **Matthew 1:1-17** for the genealogy of Jesus through the line of Judah, the blessed son of Jacob.

Lesson 12 (pp. 86-94)   Pharaoh's Invitation

Facts to Know

Field of Machpelah	burial plot of patriarchs and their wives
piece of silver	silver coin
embalm	to preserve a dead body using resins, minerals, and herbs
caravan	a train of pack animals (camels, mules)

12 sons of Jacob, fathers of the 12 tribes of Israel:

Reuben	Gad
Simeon	Asher
Levi	Dan
Judah	Naphthali
Issachar	Joseph
Zebulun	Benjamin

Memory Verse

Genesis 50:25

And Joseph took an oath of the children of Israel saying, God will surely visit you and ye shall carry up my bones from hence.

1. What does "took an oath of the children of Israel" mean?
   He made the children of Israel promise.

2. Where did Joseph die?
   Egypt

3. What does "God will surely visit you" mean?
   God had told Jacob in his dream that He would bring them out of the land of Egypt (God will surely visit you) to the land of their fathers, Abraham, Isaac, and Jacob.

4. Why did Joseph want his brothers to "carry up [his] bones from hence"?
   Joseph wanted to return to the land of his fathers and be buried with them when the children of Israel left Egypt.

44

Vocabulary and Expressions

1. **hence:** *archaic word for* from now, from this time
2. **burial plot:** land set aside for one's final resting place
3. **resins:** liquids made from plants, used for preservation or medicinal purposes

Jacob's Dream; Famine   Genesis 45-50

Comprehension Questions

1. What promise did Pharaoh make to Joseph's family?

   Pharaoh promised to give the family the best of the land of Egypt. (p. 86)

2. What gifts did Joseph give to his brothers before they left? To Benjamin?

   Joseph gave wagons, provisions for the journey, and changes of clothes. To Benjamin
   he gave 300 pieces of silver and five changes of clothes. (p. 86)

3. What did God tell Jacob in his dream?

   I will establish you as a great nation in Egypt, and I will bring you back again to your
   own land. (p. 88)

4. How did Pharaoh come to own everything in Egypt when Joseph was ruler during the famine?

   In order to eat, the people first sold their animals to Joseph, and part of their land, and
   then themselves as slaves. He gave the people seed to plant; they could keep 4/5 and
   must give 1/5 of their crop to Pharaoh. Only the priests still owned land. (pp. 90-91)

5. Where did Jacob beg to be buried? Why?

   Jacob asked Joseph to take his body back to the land of his fathers and to bury
   him where Abraham, Sarah, Isaac, Rebekah, and Leah were buried, in the cave of
   Machpelah. (p. 93)

6. When Jacob gathered his sons around him for his final blessing before he died, what did
   he foretell about their future?

   He told them that the twelve tribes of Israel would descend from them, and that Judah
   would be the one that all the others would praise and bow before.

7. Find on Unit 3 Map: ☐ Egypt   ☐ Beersheba   ☐ Nile River   ☐ Nile Delta
   ☐ Goshen   ☐ Sinai Peninsula   ☐ Gulf of Suez

45

Activities

pp. 86-87   Describe what is happening.
             Pharaoh is inviting Joseph's brothers to come to Egypt to live. He is promising to give them the
             best of the land of Egypt. Joseph is giving Benjamin 300 pieces of silver, and he is preparing 20
             donkeys loaded with corn, food, and good things from Egypt to send to his father, Jacob.

pp. 88-89   Who are the three figures in the center of the picture? What is the setting?
             Joseph and Benjamin greet their father Jacob in the land of Goshen.

pp. 90-91   What is happening in the bottom picture? in the top picture?
             In the bottom picture, the Egyptians are bringing their cattle in exchange for food. In the top
             picture, they have nothing to offer but themselves and their land for food.

pp. 92-94   What is in the wagon? Who was in the caravan and where were they going?
             What is the object on page 94?
             Jacob's coffin. Jacob's family, servants of Pharaoh, went in a caravan to bury Jacob in Canaan, in
             the Cave of Machpelah. Joseph's coffin.

Lesson 13

Background and Summary

The text of Exodus opens in much the same way Genesis begins. The people of God are enjoying life in a sort of paradise in Egypt until their fortunes take a turn for the worse. Under the leadership of pharaohs who do not know the blessings that Joseph brought Egypt, we see another struggle arise for God's people.

Egypt's policy against the Hebrews exacts slave labor from them and attempts to control their population by demanding infanticide for male Hebrew babies. This policy represents not only a threat against the nation of Israel, but also a threat against the people of God, since God has extended His special promise to the fathers of Israel.

Amid the backdrop of the struggle between the Egyptians and the sons of God, Exodus 2 proclaims the birth of a son, Moses. The hopes of a people rest on the promise of a son rescued by the special provision of God (Ex. 2:3-10). In the midst of utter despair, God brings hope and keeps His promise.

The early life of Moses, however, does not seem to hold much promise. We see a murder, a cover-up, a desperate escape, and an exile. But the Lord had much more in store for this unlikely hero.

Selected Reading:

Hebrews 11:23-26 for the role faith played in Moses' early life. Faith led Moses' parents to hide him from the Egyptians, and faith led Moses to see the delights of Egyptian royalty as less valuable than identification with God's people.

Lesson 13 (pp. 96-101)   Birth of Moses
Facts to Know

Exodus	1400 B.C., Israelites leave Egypt
Levi	Moses' tribe; became the priests of the new nation of the Israelites
Moses	led the Israelites in the Exodus; name means "drawn out"
Pharaoh's daughter	raised Moses as her own son
Midian	Moses went to live here after escaping from Pharaoh
Zipporah	Moses' wife

Memory Verse

Exodus 1:8

Now there arose up a new king over Egypt who knew not Joseph.

1. What does the expression "knew not Joseph" mean?
   The king was not aware of all the good that Joseph had done in Egypt.

2. What did the new king do to the Israelites?
   The Pharaoh put taskmasters over the Hebrews and forced them into hard labor.

46

Vocabulary and Expressions

1. **oppress**: to torment; to burden; to afflict
2. **bulrushes**: marsh reeds
3. **pitch**: tar or sap residue, used for waterproofing
4. **midwife**: a woman who delivers babies
5. **troughs**: large containers for feeding livestock

Teacher Notes

Do not be surprised if you see dates for the Exodus closer to 1200 B.C. in other texts. Scholars continue to debate the evidence in support of either 1446 B.C. or 1275 B.C., without a definitive conclusion in sight. We have selected the more traditional date of 1400 B.C. for the purposes of this study. Remember that debate over the date does not make the event any less real or significant. It took place even though we are not precisely sure when.

Moses in Midian   Exodus 1-2

Comprehension Questions

1. Why did Pharaoh fear the children of Israel in Egypt?

   Their numbers had grown so much that Pharaoh feared they would join his enemies

   and fight against him in times of war. (p. 96)

2. What did Pharaoh order midwives to do to Hebrew sons?

   He ordered the midwives attending Hebrew mothers to kill all male babies. (p. 96)

3. What did Pharaoh next command to be done with Hebrew sons?

   Pharaoh ordered that they be cast into the river (Nile). (p. 96)

4. Who found Moses in the river? What does his name mean?

   Pharaoh's daughter found Moses. His name means "drawn out" because she took him

   from the river. (p. 98)

5. Who nursed Moses until he was given to Pharaoh's daughter?

   Moses' mother, whom Pharaoh's daughter thought was a Hebrew nurse, cared for

   Moses as an infant. (p. 99)

6. Why did Moses flee from Egypt?

   One day as Moses was watching the Hebrews work, he became angry and killed a

   taskmaster who was striking one of his kinsmen. When Pharaoh heard of this, he

   sought to kill Moses. So, Moses had to flee from Egypt. (p. 100)

7. Where did Moses settle and why?

   Moses settled in the land of Midian because he met the Midian priest who took him

   in and gave his daughter for a wife. Moses tended the flocks of his father-in-law.

8. Find on Unit 3 Map: ☐ Gulf of Suez   ☐ Gulf of Aqaba   ☐ Goshen   ☐ Midian

47

BOOKS OF OLD TESTAMENT
Teach book "subtitles" listed in Teacher Guidelines.

Review:
- **Genesis**
- **Exodus**
- **Leviticus**
- **Numbers**
- **Deuteronomy**
- **Joshua**
- **Judges**
- **Ruth**
- **I & II Samuel**
- **I & II Kings**
- **I & II Chronicles**
- **Ezra**
- **Nehemiah**
- **Esther**

Teach:
- **Job**
- **Psalms**
- **Proverbs**
- **Ecclesiastes**
- **Song of Solomon**

Activities

p. 97   Who is doing the work in the picture and why? What are they building? How can you tell
            who the Pharaoh is? What are the taskmasters doing?
            The children of Israel are being oppressed because Pharaoh fears their numbers. They are
            building the cities of Pithom and Ramses. Pharaoh always wears the distinctive head piece. The
            taskmasters are beating the children of Israel.

pp. 98-98   Identify Moses, Pharaoh's daughter, and Moses' sister. What are the plants growing by the side
            of the water?   The plants are bulrushes.

pp. 100-101 How can you identify Moses? How many women are there? Who are they? How has
            Moses helped them?   Moses is still wearing an Egyptian headdress. The seven women are the
            seven daughters of the priest of Midian. Moses helped them water their flocks and protected
            them from the shepherds trying to drive them away from the well.

Moses is a biblical hero hidden in youth. Can you name the mythological heroes hidden in youth?
            Romulus and Remus, Zeus, Perseus, Theseus, Oedipus, Jason, and Heracles.

Memory Verse Review: #22 in Appendix.

Lesson 14

Background and Summary

The account of the burning bush highlights two features of the story. First, God is faithful to His promise; He inclines His ear to the sufferings of His people and remembers the pledge of His covenant (Ex. 2:23-25, 3:6-9). Just as in Jacob's dream, the Lord introduces himself as the God of his fathers, the God of Abraham, Isaac, and Jacob. The only God that Moses knows is the God of the Hebrews, the God of his ancestors. In this, we know that our God is not an abstract or impersonal deity, but rather, He has relationships with His people. Thus, by faith, He is the God of our fathers too.

Second, Moses is a reluctant, unlikely champion of God's salvation. He is riddled with doubt and questions God's calling him to be the messenger (Ex. 3:11; 4:1,10). In response to the weakness of His prophet, the Lord assures Moses that if Pharaoh will not fear the messenger, he will learn to fear the God named "I am who I am." In this way, God is determined to bring about the redemption of Israel promised beforehand to Abraham (Gen. 15:13-14). To help, God gives Moses wondrous signs that will teach Moses to trust the great strength of the Lord and also get Pharaoh's attention. Again, God elects to use the weak vessels of this world to magnify His strength (I Cor. 1:26-27).

Selected Readings:
- **Genesis 15:13-14** for God's promise to Abraham to bring his descendants back from the land of captivity.
- **Genesis 28:13** for God's same introduction of himself as "the God of our fathers" in Jacob's dream.
- **Acts 7:20-36** for a commentary in Stephen's sermon about how God used Moses in Salvation History.
- **I Corinthians 1:25, 26-27** for Paul's encouragement about God using the weak things of this world to display His great strength.
- **John 8:58** for Jesus declaring his equal divinity with God by using the "I am" saying from Exodus 3:14.

Lesson 14 (pp. 102-105)   God Calls Moses

Facts to Know

Aaron	spokesman for his brother Moses
Yahweh	God's real name that was revealed to Moses by God Himself; means "I AM" or "HE WHO IS" in Hebrew
Jehoveh	English for **Yahweh**
Mount Horeb	where God spoke to Moses in the burning bush
Miriam	sister of Moses and Aaron

Memory Verse

Exodus 3:13-14

And Moses said unto God,
    Behold, when I come unto the children of Israel and shall say unto them, the God of your fathers has sent me to you and they shall say unto me, What is his name? What shall I say unto them?
And God said unto Moses,
    I AM THAT I AM;
and He said,
    Thus shall you say unto the children of Israel, I AM hath sent me unto you.

1. Give the Hebrew and English names for God and what they mean.
   The Hebrew **Yahweh** and English **Jehoveh** mean I AM or I AM HE WHO IS, or I AM THAT I AM.

2. God's real name describes his most important attribute. What is it?
   Existence. Everything that exists comes from God and exists in Him and by His power.

48

Vocabulary and Expressions

1. **kinsman**: relative and family member
2. **taskmaster**: slave driver; work foreman
3. **land flowing with milk and honey**: Canaan, the Promised Land
4. **Yahweh** (ya **way**): the divine name of God, transliterated from Hebrew
5. **leprous**: having to do with leprosy, a skin disease that deteriorates flesh

The Miraculous Signs   Exodus 2-4

Comprehension Questions

1. How did the angel of the Lord appear to Moses?

    The angel of the Lord appeared in a burning bush that was not consumed. (p. 102)

2. How did God first identify Himself to Moses?

    God told Moses that He was the God of his fathers, the God of Abraham, Isaac, and Jacob. (p. 102)

3. What message did God give Moses?

    He had come to deliver the Hebrews from slavery in Egypt and bring them to the Promised Land. God said that Moses was to go to Pharaoh and tell him. (p. 103)

4. How did Moses respond to God's calling?

    Moses had many questions and excuses. He asked to know God's name, and he asked what to do if the children of Israel did not believe him.

5. What miraculous signs did God give Moses?

    a. God turned Moses' shepherd's rod into a snake and back again.

    b. He made Moses' hand appear leprous and then normal again. (p. 104)

6. What was Moses' last excuse?

    Moses protested that he was slow of speech. (p. 104)

7. Who did God give Moses to aid him with speech?

    God sent Moses' brother Aaron to help him with his speech. (p. 104)

8. Find on Unit 3 Map: ☐ Midian ☐ Mt. Horeb (Mt. Sinai)

49

Teacher Notes

In this lesson, the revelation of God's name teaches us a very important truth about how we should think about God. By calling Himself "I am that I am," the Lord is saying that His nature or character should be defined by His existence or being. Consider the Latin verb **sum**. **Sum** is a verb of being that states, "I am." The Lord makes the same statement in Hebrew when He calls Himself "Yahweh." Because He is who He is, there is no further explanation needed. Just as Saint Paul said to the men of Athens in Acts 17, He is before all things and in Him all things have their being. For such a magnificent and incomparable God, His very existence remains the measure of His person. Therefore, the best way to communicate His nature to us was to say, "I am the one who is."

Activities

pp. 102-103   What is Moses doing? Where are his shoes? Why? How does Moses look different on the previous page? Why?
Moses stopped to see why the bush was on fire but not burning. God told him from the bush to "take off your shoes because the land on which you are standing is holy ground." Moses looked like an Egyptian, but now he looks like a shepherd.

p. 104   What is happening?
Moses' shepherd's rod has been turned into a snake.

p. 105   Who is speaking? Who is standing next to him? Why?
Aaron is speaking to the elders of Israel, and Moses is standing next to him. Aaron speaks for Moses, and Moses speaks for God.

Memory Verse Review: #23-25 in Appendix.

Lesson 15

Background and Summary

As anticipated, when Moses and Aaron go before Pharaoh, he rejects vehemently their claim on his nation of slaves. Egypt is the great superpower in the Ancient Near East, and the pride of Pharaoh has no end. He asks Moses, "Who is the Lord that I should obey his voice to let Israel go?" (Ex. 5:3).

The narrative of the Ten Plagues will answer Pharaoh's question definitively (Ex. 7:14-11). God will demonstrate in power that He alone rules the earth and defends His "son," the chosen people of Israel (Ex. 4:22). In increasing the hardships of the people and continuing to reject the commands of God through Moses, Pharaoh evidences the fact that God has hardened his heart to reject the Lord. The obstinacy of Pharaoh, however, is part of God's plan to magnify His power before the people (Ex. 7:3-5, 13, and 22).

Pharaoh's hardened heart displays for us an alarming example of how a person can continue rejecting the Lord until his heart becomes so callous to the call of God that there remains no hope for him. Remember that hearts become hardened through making a practice of sin.

Selected Readings:
- **Psalm 135:1-9** for Israel's song of praise about God's mighty acts in Egypt. God is celebrated as the sovereign creator of the earth and the supreme ruler of the nations.
- **Romans 9:17** for Paul's statement about Pharaoh and his hard heart.

Lesson 15 (pp. 106-111)   Pharaoh and the Israelites

Facts to Know

Pharaoh	name of Egyptian kings
plague	a widespread, destructive outbreak
enchantment	magic spell

Memory Verse

Exodus 7:3

And I will harden Pharaoh's heart, and multiply my signs and my wonders in the land of Egypt.

1. What does "harden Pharaoh's heart" mean?
The expression means to allow Pharaoh to remain unwilling to listen and not have a change of heart. Pharaoh's pattern of habitual sin caused his heart to become too hard to yield to God.

2. Why did God harden Pharaoh's heart?
God hardened Pharaoh's heart so He could show that He is the true God in the land of Egypt by the number and power of His miracles.

50

Vocabulary and Expressions

1. **idle**: lazy or inactive
2. **feast**: banquet or larger dinner
3. **bricks**: building material made from baking mud and straw
4. **sorcerer**: one who practices witchcraft and divination
5. **magician**: one who casts spells and performs tricks of illusion

The Ten Plagues   Exodus 5-8

Comprehension Questions

1. What message did God send to Pharaoh through Moses and Aaron?

   "Let my people go that they may worship me in the wilderness." (p. 106)

2. What was Pharaoh's response to the message of Moses and Aaron?

   Pharaoh asked, "Who is this God that Pharaoh should obey his voice?"

3. How did Pharaoh punish the Hebrews because of the message of Moses and Aaron?

   Pharaoh punished the children of Israel by giving them more work. They had to find

   their own straw to make bricks, but make just as many bricks as when the straw was

   given to them. (p. 106)

4. How old were Moses and Aaron when called to lead the Exodus?

   Moses was 80; Aaron was 83. (p. 108)

5. How did Pharaoh rebuke the miracle of the rod performed by Aaron?

   Pharaoh had his own magicians perform the same trick. (p. 108)

6. What were the first three plagues God sent upon the Egyptians?

   The first three plagues were the plague upon the river (plague of water and blood), the

   plague of frogs, and the plague of lice. (p. 110)

7. Which was the first miracle the magicians of Pharaoh could not imitate?

   The magicians could not imitate the plague of lice. (p. 111)

8. Find on Unit 3 Map: ☐ Midian ☐ Mt. Horeb (Sinai) ☐ Canaan ☐ Goshen

   ☐ Sinai Peninsula ☐ Gulf of Suez ☐ Gulf of Aqaba ☐ Red Sea

51

BOOKS OF OLD TESTAMENT
Teach book "subtitles" listed in
Teacher Guidelines.

Review:
- **Genesis**
- **Exodus**
- **Leviticus**
- **Numbers**
- **Deuteronomy**
- **Joshua**
- **Judges**
- **Ruth**
- **I & II Samuel**
- **I & II Kings**
- **I & II Chronicles**
- **Ezra**
- **Nehemiah**
- **Esther**
- **Job**
- **Psalms**
- **Proverbs**
- **Ecclesiastes**
- **Song of Solomon**

Activities

p. 107   What are the children of Israel doing?

               They are gathering straw to make bricks while the taskmasters oppress them.

p. 108   Identify Pharaoh, the magicians, and Aaron. What is happening?

               Aaron is in the forefront, facing Pharaoh, whose magicians are beside and around him. Aaron's
               serpent is swallowing the serpents of Pharaoh's magicians.

pp. 110-111   What are the Egyptians doing?

               The Egyptians are cleaning up the frogs from the second plague.

Memory Verse Review: #26 in Appendix.

Review Lesson: Unit 3

Instructions

Use this Review Lesson to support mastery of the material presented in the previous five lessons. Drill the Facts to Know orally or have a Facts to Know Bee. Places to Know should be identified on the maps in this lesson. Events to Know will be reviewed in the timeline exercise which follows. Students may work independently on these two pages of the Review, but answers should be checked in class. A test for this unit is included in the back of this book.

Review Lesson: Unit 3 (Lessons 11-15)

Events to Know in Salvation History

The Exodus
A Baby Afloat on the Nile
The Murderer Flees
Exile in Midian
The Burning Bush
A Hard Heart
The Ten Plagues

People to Know
Pharaoh's Daughter
Moses
Zipporah
Aaron
Pharaoh
Miriam

Words to Know
yearn: to wish for or want
embalm: to preserve a dead body
caravan: a train of pack animals
midwife: a woman who delivers babies
Yahweh: Hebrew "I am," name for God
enchantment: magic spell
plague: a widespread, destructive outbreak

Places to Know
Egypt
Goshen
Midian
Canaan
Beersheba
Mt. Horeb (Sinai)
Sinai Peninsula
Nile River
Nile Delta
Red Sea
Mediterranean Sea
Dead Sea
Gulf of Suez
Gulf of Aqaba

Names for People of God
The Chosen People
Hebrews
The Children of Israel
Israelites

Books of the O.T.
5-12-5-5
Genesis
Exodus
Leviticus
Numbers
Deuteronomy

Joshua
Judges
Ruth
I II Samuel
I II Kings
I II Chronicles
Ezra
Nehemiah
Esther

Job
Psalms
Proverbs
Ecclesiastes
Song of Solomon

Name Meanings Review

Eve	mother of all living
Abraham	father of nations
Sarah	mother of nations and kings
Isaac	he who laughs
Judah	I will praise
Moses	drawn out

Twelve Tribes of Israel
Reuben
Simeon
Levi
Judah
Issachar
Zebulun
Gad
Asher
Dan
Naphthali
Joseph
Benjamin

52

Review Lesson: Unit 3 (Lessons 11-15)

Give the corresponding word or phrase:

1. Moses' sister _____ Miriam _____
2. Moses' brother _____ Aaron _____
3. After killing an Egyptian, Moses fled to _____ Midian _____
4. The Hebrew name for God _____ Yahweh _____
5. The part of Egypt Pharaoh gave to Joseph's family Goshen _____
6. What does Yahweh mean? _____ "I am" _____
7. What was found in Benjamin's sack? _____ silver cup _____
8. He was hidden in a basket on the Nile _____ Moses _____
9. How did the angel of the Lord appear to Moses on Mt. Horeb? _a burning bush_
10. Jacob prophesied this tribe would rule the others _____ Judah _____
11. The Nile empties into what sea? _____ Mediterranean _____
12. Which direction does the Nile flow? _____ north _____
13. What is the great river of Egypt? _____ Nile _____
14. The arc of land stretching from the Persian Gulf to Egypt _____ Fertile Crescent
15. Three names for God's people _____ Israel, Hebrews, Children of Israel
16. The Children of Israel built these two cities for Pharaoh __ Pithom and Ramses
17. The tribe of Moses and Aaron _____ Levi _____
18. The departure of Israel from Egypt in 1400 B.C. _Exodus_

Match each name with its meaning:

D	Eve	A. I will praise
F	Abraham	B. mother of nations and kings
B	Sarah	C. drawn out
E	Isaac	D. mother of all living
A	Judah	E. he who laughs
C	Moses	F. father of nations

Match up the vocabulary words:

E	plague	A. a train of pack animals
F	embalm	B. a woman who delivers babies
A	caravan	C. magic spell
B	midwife	D. to wish for or want
D	yearn	E. a widespread, destructive outbreak
C	enchantment	F. to preserve a dead body

53

Old Testament Drill Questions

All of the short answer review questions from each Review Lesson have been compiled in Appendix 2. Continue to review them throughout the year. They are great for bees and competitions.

Review Lesson: Unit 3

Timeline Review

Elementary-age children do not have a well-developed sense of time, especially time long ago and time over a long period. Putting events and people in order is also an advanced skill. These timelines are designed to teach beginning skills in creating a mental timeline of history. Students cannot do this work independently; this is a teacher-directed learning activity. Review the names Prehistory, Patriarchs, and Exodus, and the dates and people belonging to those periods. Next, go to "The Exodus" and number the events in order and then complete the timeline.

Review Lesson: Unit 3 (Lessons 11-15)

Salvation History Timeline

The events of Salvation History are out of order! Number them in correct order. Then match people from the Review Lesson with events. Some people may be used more than once and in different combinations than shown in the list. Add the first two periods of Salvation History and their dates. You can find them in the previous two Review Lessons.

The Exodus

4	The Burning Bush
1	A Baby Afloat on the Nile
3	Exile in Midian
2	The Murderer Flees
6	The Ten Plagues
5	A Hard Heart

People

Pharaoh's Daughter
Moses
Zipporah
Aaron
Pharaoh

Date	Events	Period	People
Time Begins		Prehistory	
2000 B.C.		Patriarchs	
1400 B.C.		Exodus	
	A Baby Afloat on the Nile		Moses, Pharaoh's Daughter
	The Murderer Flees		Moses
	Exile in Midian		Moses, Zipporah
	The Burning Bush		Moses, Aaron
	A Hard Heart		Pharaoh
	The Ten Plagues		

54

Review Lesson: Unit 3 (Lessons 11-15)

Scripture Memorization

Check each box if you can recite the Scripture verse from memory. Write each from memory or teacher dictation. Be accurate.

☐ **Genesis 45:4, 5, 8** _____

I am Joseph your brother, whom ye sold into Egypt. Now therefore be not grieved with

yourselves, for it was not you that sent me hither, but God. _____

☐ **Genesis 50:25** _____

And Joseph took an oath of the children of Israel, saying, God will surely visit you and

ye shall carry up my bones from hence. _____

☐ **Exodus 1:8** _____

Now there arose up a new king over Egypt who knew not Joseph. _____

☐ **Exodus 3:13-14** _____

And Moses said unto God, _____

Behold, when I come unto the children of Israel and shall say unto them, the God of

your fathers has sent me to you and they shall say unto me, What is his name? What

shall I say unto them?

And God said unto Moses, I AM THAT I AM; and He said, Thus shall you say unto the

children of Israel, I AM hath sent me unto you. _____

_____

_____

_____

☐ **Exodus 7:3** _____

And I will harden Pharaoh's heart, and multiply my signs and my wonders in the land

of Egypt. _____

55

Review Lesson: Unit 3

Memory Verses

To recite memory verses, give the first few words and let students complete the verse orally. Students may write the verse from memory, from dictation, or copy it.

Review Lesson: Unit 3

Books of the Old Testament (partial list)

The Books of the Law

1. Genesis
2. Exodus
3. Leviticus
4. Numbers
5. Deuteronomy

The Books of History

1. Joshua
2. Judges
3. Ruth
4. I Samuel
5. II Samuel
6. I Kings
7. II Kings
8. I Chronicles
9. II Chronicles
10. Ezra
11. Nehemiah
12. Esther

The Books of Wisdom

1. Job
2. Psalms
3. Proverbs
4. Ecclesiastes
5. Song of Solomon

56

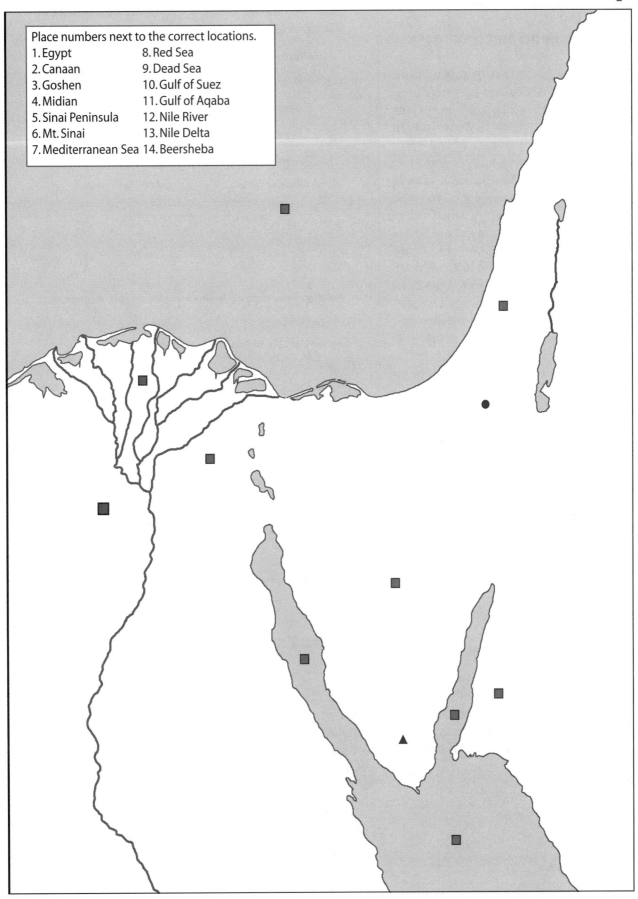

Place numbers next to the correct locations.
1. Egypt   8. Red Sea
2. Canaan   9. Dead Sea
3. Goshen   10. Gulf of Suez
4. Midian   11. Gulf of Aqaba
5. Sinai Peninsula 12. Nile River
6. Mt. Sinai   13. Nile Delta
7. Mediterranean Sea 14. Beersheba

Lesson 16

Background and Summary

With plague after plague, God demonstrates His rule over the creation. The party tricks of Pharaoh's magicians pale in comparison to God's sovereign control over the elements of the earth He made.

Unfortunately, though, each plague results in the same defiance; Pharaoh can not admit the power of Israel's God. His hard heart rejects God's claim on the Hebrew people. In this power struggle, God must assert His claim in an ultimate way (Ex. 11:6). By striking the firstborn sons of Egypt, God completes His plan to humble the greatest of nations and bring about the release of His people (Ex. 12:29-32).

Reluctant but humiliated, Pharaoh can no longer oppose the God of Israel.

Facts to Know

The Ten Plagues:

Plague of Water and Blood	Plague of Sores
Plague of Frogs	Plague of Hail and Fire
Plague of Lice	Plague of Locusts
Plague of Flies	Plague of Darkness
Plague of Cattle	Death of the Firstborn

Memory Verse

Exodus 12:13

And when I see the blood, I will pass over you, and the plague shall not be upon you, when I smite the land of Egypt.

1. What does "smite" mean? Smite means "to kill."

2. What religious holiday is associated with the plague of the firstborn?
Passover, or the Feast of Unleavened Bread, begins the Hebrew calendar year and commemorates for Israel the plague of the firstborn when Yahweh "passed over" and spared the firstborn children of Israel.

3. Why did the angel of Death pass over the houses of the Hebrews?
The Hebrews were commanded to mark their lintel and door posts with lamb's blood as a sign that the family inside feared the Lord.

60

Vocabulary and Expressions

1. **swarm**: cloud; mass; flock
2. **vile**: wicked or depraved
3. **abomination**: disgrace; scandal; atrocity
4. **firstborn**: heir of blessing; the favored son of the family
5. **maidservant**: female slave

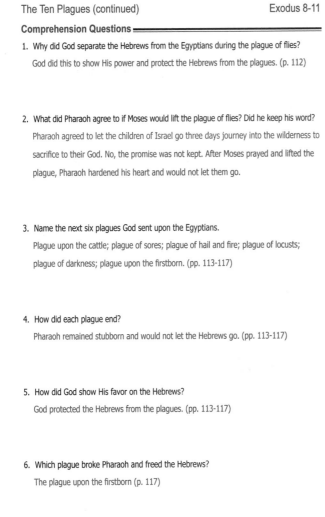

The Ten Plagues (continued)   Exodus 8-11

Comprehension Questions

1. Why did God separate the Hebrews from the Egyptians during the plague of flies?

   God did this to show His power and protect the Hebrews from the plagues. (p. 112)

2. What did Pharaoh agree to if Moses would lift the plague of flies? Did he keep his word?

   Pharaoh agreed to let the children of Israel go three days journey into the wilderness to
   sacrifice to their God. No, the promise was not kept. After Moses prayed and lifted the
   plague, Pharaoh hardened his heart and would not let them go.

3. Name the next six plagues God sent upon the Egyptians.

   Plague upon the cattle; plague of sores; plague of hail and fire; plague of locusts;
   plague of darkness; plague upon the firstborn. (pp. 113-117)

4. How did each plague end?

   Pharaoh remained stubborn and would not let the Hebrews go. (pp. 113-117)

5. How did God show His favor on the Hebrews?

   God protected the Hebrews from the plagues. (pp. 113-117)

6. Which plague broke Pharaoh and freed the Hebrews?

   The plague upon the firstborn (p. 117)

61

Lesson 16

BOOKS OF OLD TESTAMENT
Teach book "subtitles" listed in
Teacher Guidelines.

Review:
- **Genesis**
- **Exodus**
- **Leviticus**
- **Numbers**
- **Deuteronomy**
- **Joshua**
- **Judges**
- **Ruth**
- **I & II Samuel**
- **I & II Kings**
- **I & II Chronicles**
- **Ezra**
- **Nehemiah**
- **Esther**
- **Job**
- **Psalms**
- **Proverbs**
- **Ecclesiastes**
- **Song of Solomon**

Teach:
- **Isaiah**
- **Jeremiah**
- **Lamentations**
- **Ezekiel**
- **Daniel**

Activities

Name the plague on these pages:

p. 112   The plague of flies

p. 113   The plague of cattle

p. 114   The plague of hail and fire

pp. 116-117   The plague of locusts

Lesson 17

Background and Summary

Before the Lord leads His people out of captivity in Egypt, He institutes the Passover ceremony so that His people will never forget how miraculously their God rescued them from slavery. Celebrated with the Feast of Unleavened Bread, the Passover meal symbolizes the exit the people were about to make out of Egypt. They do not even have time to wait for the yeast in their bread to rise.

As the spirit of the Lord goes out through all of Egypt, God pours out judgment on the land. Unless the door frame of a house is marked by the blood of the Passover lamb, the spirit of the Lord will strike down the firstborn of that house. This prefigures the sacrifice of Christ as the Lamb of God that covers over the sins of His people, saving them from the judgment of God. With the lamb and with Christ, we see that God's mercy always comes at a cost.

When the Israelites finally leave Egypt, Pharaoh's bitter heart sends him after the people. With the sea at their feet and Pharaoh's army on their backs, the Israelites begin to question God's plan for their rescue. God has a twofold purpose in the crossing of the Red Sea. First, He effectively annihilates the Egyptian army when they follow Israel's path, for "there remained not so much as one of them" (Ex. 14:23-28). Second, He demonstrates His might to the people, who fear and trust Him afterward (Ex. 14:31).

Selected Readings:

- **Leviticus 23:4-8** for laws concerning the celebration of the Passover and the Feast of Unleavened Bread in Israel.
- **John 13:1** for witness to the convergence of Jesus' crucifixion and the Passover.
- **I Corinthians 5:7** for Paul's statement about Jesus as the Passover lamb.
- **Isaiah 53:7** for Isaiah's prophecy about the Messiah as a sacrificial lamb.
- **Exodus 15:1-18, 21** for a song of praise after crossing the sea on dry land.
- **Psalm 136:1-16** for a song of praise about God's mighty acts in saving Israel from the Egyptian pursuit.

Lesson 17 (pp. 118-123)   Night of the Passover

Facts to Know

Passover	feast to celebrate the Exodus when the angel of Death passed over the houses of the Hebrews
unleavened bread	bread without yeast; served at Passover
Miriam	sister of Moses and Aaron; prophetess
timbrel	musical instrument like a tambourine, but without the parchment

Memory Verse

Exodus 15:1

Then sang Moses and the children of Israel:
    I will sing unto the Lord
    For he hath triumphed gloriously
    The horse and his rider
    Hath he thrown into the sea.

1. What was the occasion for this song of celebration?
   The safe crossing of the Red Sea and the destruction of the Egyptian cavalry was cause for celebration.

2. Who is the horse and his rider?
   The Egyptian horsemen and charioteers.

3. What sea is referred to in this verse?
   Red Sea

62

Teacher Notes
Red Sea or Sea of Reeds

Since the time of the Septuagint (the Greek translation of the Old Testament), many people have thought the body of water Israel crossed to be the Red Sea. The original language of the text, however, is better translated "sea of reeds." Thus, the sea of reeds rules out both arms of the Red Sea, the Gulf of Suez and Aqaba, since these are saltwater bodies not conducive to the growth of freshwater reeds. Rather, scholars suggest one of the several lakes in the Nile Delta area. Possible alternate locations would include the following lakes: Menzaleh, Ballah, Timsah, Sirbonis, or the Bitter Lakes.

Crossing of the Red Sea   Exodus 12-15

Comprehension Questions

1. How did the Israelites mark their homes so they were not victims of the plague of firstborn?

   They marked the top and side posts of their doorways with lamb's blood. (p. 118)

2. What did the children of Israel eat the night of the Passover?

   They roasted a lamb and ate the meat with unleavened bread and bitter herbs. They could not wait for the leaven in the bread to rise because they were to be ready to leave in haste.

3. How many Israelites fled from Egypt? How long had they lived in Egypt?

   600,000, not counting children, fled Egypt after living there 430 years. (p. 119)

4. How did God assist His people during their journey?

   God gave them a pillar of cloud to show the way by day and a pillar of fire by night. (p. 120)

5. How were the Israelites rescued by the hand of God at the Red Sea?

   God parted the waters of the Red Sea, leaving a passage of dry land. (p. 121)

6. What happened to the Egyptians who were chasing them?

   The waters closed back over the Egyptians and drowned them all. (p. 122)

7. Find on Unit 4 Map: ☐ Red Sea ☐ Gulf of Suez ☐ Gulf of Aqaba ☐ Sinai Peninsula ☐ Nile River ☐ Nile Delta ☐ Goshen

63

Activities

pp. 118-119   For what are the people preparing? What did preparations include?
The people are preparing for Passover; they are preparing the Passover lamb, unleavened bread, and bitter herbs. They have also sprinkled blood on their door posts.

p. 120   What happened to the Egyptian horses and chariots?
The Egyptian horsemen and charioteers were drowned in the sea.

p. 122   Who are these women? What are they singing? What are their instruments?
The women of Israel are singing with timbrels, celebrating the defeat of the armies of the Egyptians who were drowned in the Red Sea.

Draw a picture of the Israelites passing through the Red Sea on dry land.

Lesson 18

Background and Summary

Three days after the miraculous events at the Red Sea, the Israelites begin grumbling against the Lord and His servant Moses. The long journey ahead of the Israelites will definitely test their faithfulness and loyalty to the God that rescued them from the house of bondage in Egypt. Already, in Exodus 15-17, they doubt the Lord's ability to provide for their most basic needs: food and water. In their murmuring, they even declare that it would have been better to have stayed in Egypt as slaves where they could have eaten their fill of bread and meat instead of dying of hunger in the wilderness (Ex. 16:2-3).

We must note how quickly the people lose sight of the amazing ways God saved them in view of worrying about their appetites. As we read their story, we are quick to criticize the Israelites, but we too are often guilty of such a short-sighted view of God's provision and care. We can show this same selfish spirit each day if we do not allow the testimony of God's goodness to shape the way we consider our present concerns and worries. The spiritual lesson here centers on the decision to have a grumbling heart or a grateful heart.

Keep in mind, however, that despite the Israelites' complaining, God shows His grace once again, making bitter waters sweet, raining food on the ground, and issuing water from a rock.

Selected Readings:

- **Psalm 76** recounts the rescue from Egypt to the kingship of David. See **76:12-29** for the song about God feeding Israel in the wilderness.
- **Joshua 5:12** for where the manna ends after the Israelites taste the first fruits of the Promised Land.
- **John 6:31-35, 58** for how Jesus is the "Bread of Life," better than manna. The manna of the Old Testament foreshadows Jesus as the Bread of Life.
- **I Corinthians 10:1-6** for the warning to avoid the mistakes of Israel in the wilderness when they obeyed their sinful appetites more than they feared the Lord.

Facts to Know

Marah	means "bitterness"; a place of rest on the Exodus
manna	bread provided by God during the Wilderness Wanderings
omer	one-tenth bushel of bread
Massah	means "temptation"; where Moses struck the rock and water poured out

Memory Verse

Exodus 16:4

Then the Lord said to Moses, Behold I will rain bread from heaven for you.

1. Why did the Lord always speak to Moses?
   He was the leader of the Israelites.

2. Why did the Lord always answer the needs of the Israelites?
   The Lord had promised to deliver them.

3. What does "behold" mean?   to observe; to look

4. The word "behold" is usually used to announce a ____miracle____.

64

Vocabulary and Expressions

1. **Hebrews, Children of Israel,** and **Israelites:** names used interchangeably for the people of God and descendants of Abraham's promise
2. **murmur:** to complain, grumble, or whine
3. **quail:** small ground fowl (tastes like chicken)
4. **coriander seed:** Old World herb that produced small white seeds that could be ground or used whole for seasoning dishes
5. **wafer:** thin, crisp cake or biscuit
6. **omer:** Old Testament unit of measurement equal to one-tenth of an ephah, about a half gallon
7. **elders:** the older men of Israel that provided leadership to their families and tribes
8. **hoarfrost:** frost

Manna from Heaven   Exodus 15-17
Comprehension Questions

1. Why did the people "murmur" against Moses at Marah? How did Moses answer them?
   The Israelites went for three days and found no water in the wilderness of Shur. When they did find water at Marah, it was bitter and unfit to drink. (p. 124) Moses cried to the Lord, who showed him a tree, which he cast into the bitter water and made it sweet.

2. Why did the people "murmur" against Moses in the Wilderness of Zin, between Sinai and Elim? What did they say?
   The people grew hungry and missed the food they had in Egypt. They said, "It would have been better for us to have died in Egypt where we had food than to die of hunger here in the wilderness."

3. How did God provide food for his people in their Wilderness Wanderings? How were they to gather the manna?
   In the evening, there were quails, and in the morning, after the dew dried, there were small particles of bread. Moses instructed them to gather an omer for each person and to not leave any for the next day. On the sixth day, they were to gather enough for two days, because on the Sabbath there would be no bread.

4. How long did the children of Israel eat manna, and how did their descendants know about the manna?
   They ate the manna for 40 years. Aaron put an omer of manna into a pot for their children to see. (p. 127)

5. Why did the people murmur at Massah? What did they say? What did Moses do?
   The people were thirsty and said, "Why did you bring us out of Egypt to die of thirst?" Moses struck the rock with his rod and water came out of the rock. (p. 129)

6. Find on Unit 4 Map: ☐ Marah ☐ Gulf of Suez ☐ Gulf of Aqaba ☐ Sinai Peninsula ☐ Elim ☐ Nile Delta ☐ Canaan

65

Continue to recite the Books of the Old Testament and begin to add the minor prophets, four at a time.

- **Hosea**
- **Joel**
- **Amos**
- **Obadiah**
- Jonah
- Micah
- Nahum
- Habakkuk
- Zephaniah
- Haggai
- Zechariah
- Malachi

Activities

p. 124   Where are the children of Israel? How do you know?
They are at Elim, where there are 12 wells and 70 palm trees.

pp. 126-127 What are the Hebrews doing?
They are gathering manna off the ground.

p. 129   Identify Moses. What is he doing? Who is with him?
Moses is striking the rock as God had told him to, in order to get water. The elders are gathered to observe the miracle.

Memory Verse Review: #27 in Appendix.

Lesson 19

Background and Summary

As the children of Israel are led through the wilderness by God, those that oppose Israel are opposed by God, and those that bless Israel are blessed by God. Such is the case with Amalek and Jethro; Israel is given supernatural assistance to defeat Amalek, and Moses is given wise counsel by Jethro, the priest of Midian.

As the people draw near to the mountain, God commands Moses to ready the people both physically and mentally for a covenant-making ceremony. First, the people are required to cleanse and purify themselves in order to meet with the Lord. Second, the Lord instructs Moses to remind the people of how and why He saved them from Egypt (Ex. 19:4-6).

The terrible imagery of this scene—the fire, smoke, lightning, and thunder—further emphasizes the importance of Israel's response to God. For such a great God, we can only respond with great faith and obedience.

Selected Reading:

Hebrews 12:18-24 for a comparison of Mt. Sinai with the heavenly mountain, Mt. Zion. Sinai, with its terrible physical displays of God's power and might, contrasts the splendor of the heavenly city in that Sinai evokes fear and trembling in the people, while Zion represents the hope of a final rest in Christ. At Sinai the law mediates between God and the people, but the mercy and grace of Christ mediates for the people in Zion.

The numbering of the Ten Commandments is another Catholic-Protestant issue. Since they are not actually numbered in Scripture, allow students to number them according to their faith tradition. (In the Catholic tradition, the last commandment is broken into two and the second is subsumed into the first.)

Lesson 19 (pp. 130-138)   Amalek; Jethro and Moses
Facts to Know

Amalek	on the way to Mt. Sinai, this king came out to fight with Israel and was defeated as long as Moses held up his hands
Rephidim	where Joshua led the Israelites against the Amalekites
Joshua	military leader and successor of Moses
Jethro	priest of Midian; Moses' father-in-law
Mount Sinai	where Moses received the Ten Commandments

Memory Verse

Exodus 20:1-17
I am the Lord thy God, which have brought thee out of the land of Egypt, out of the house of bondage.

Thou shalt have no other gods before Me.
Thou shalt not make unto thee any graven image.
Thou shalt not take the name of the Lord thy God in vain.
Remember the Sabbath, to keep it holy.
Honor thy father and thy mother.
Thou shalt not kill.
Thou shalt not commit adultery.
Thou shalt not steal.
Thou shalt not bear false witness.
Thou shalt not covet thy neighbor's wife, nor anything that is thy neighbor's.

Give the meaning of these words:

graven image	a picture or sculpture
take in vain	to use thoughtlessly or disrespectfully
Sabbath	seventh day, day of rest
covet	to desire strongly what belongs to someone else
bear false witness	to lie about someone

66

Vocabulary and Expressions

1. **house of bondage**: life of slavery in Egypt
2. **"no other gods before me"**: false gods of other peoples can never replace the solemn relationship between Yahweh and His people
3. **adultery**: unfaithfulness in a marriage

Teacher Notes

1. **capital crimes**: crimes that demand the death penalty
2. **usury**: charging interest for borrowed money, which was considered a crime. Usury at the time meant very high interest charges that kept a borrower indebted to the lender for a long time.

The Ten Commandments   Exodus 17-21

Comprehension Questions————————————————

1. How did Moses affect the battle between Joshua and Amalek?

   When Moses held up his hands, Israel was victorious. When he dropped his hands, Amalek was victorious. (p. 130)

2. How did Hur and Aaron assist Moses?

   They held Moses' hands up when he was weary. (p. 130)

3. What advice did Jethro give Moses?

   Jethro advised Moses to appoint able men as judges under him who would have the power to decide smaller matters, so that Moses would not wear himself out. (p. 132)

4. What were the instructions God set for the people to receive the Ten Commandments?

   God instructed them to assemble in clean clothes at the base of Mount Sinai, without touching it. (p. 134)

5. How did God appear to the people at the base of Sinai?

   God appeared in a thick cloud of smoke, thunder, lightning, and the sound of a trumpet on the mountain. (p. 134)

6. After the Ten Commandments, God gave some other laws to Moses for the people. What were they about?

   God offered laws regarding crimes requiring capital punishment, treatment of strangers and widows and orphans, and usury. (p. 137)

7. Find on Unit 4 Map: ☐ Midian   ☐ Elim   ☐ Marah
   ☐ Mt. Sinai   ☐ Rephidim

67

Continue to recite the Books of the Old Testament and add the next four minor prophets.

- Hosea
- Joel
- Amos
- Obadiah
- **Jonah**
- **Micah**
- **Nahum**
- **Habakkuk**
- Zephaniah
- Haggai
- Zechariah
- Malachi

Activities

p. 130   Identify Moses, Aaron, and Hur. What are they doing? Why?
           Aaron and Hur are holding up Moses' arms so the Israelites will be victorious in the battle with the Amalekites.

p. 132   Identify the two men. What are they discussing?
           Jethro has come to visit Moses and, after seeing his workload, gives him some good advice.

p. 135   Describe what is happening in the picture.
           God is appearing on Mt. Sinai in a cloud of smoke and lightning. The children of Israel are gathered at the foot of the mountain, and Moses and Joshua are going up to meet with God.

p. 136   Where is Moses? What are the stone tablets?
           Moses is on Mt. Sinai, and the stone tablets are the Ten Commandments.

Lesson 20

Background and Summary

Along with the moral and social prescriptions of God's principles set forth in the Law, Moses also receives instruction about how Israel would structure its worship of God. This component of the law we may designate the "Ceremonial Laws," which included a litany of instructions on the who, what, where, and how of Israelite worship. The attention to detail found in the ceremonial laws represents the profound perfection of their object of worship: the Lord God. A completely holy God demands completely holy worship. How gracious that God would inform Israel exactly how He was to be worshipped!

Most significant, the Ark of the Covenant (or the Ark of the Testimony) represents God's presence among His people. For Israel it functions in two ways. First, it contains sacred objects that recall the provision of God for Israel in the wilderness, such as the stone tablets, manna, the staff, etc. Second, the top of the Ark is fitted with a mercy seat, on which the priests would sprinkle the blood of the sacrifices and thereby make atonement for the sins of the people. For this reason, the Ark will prove vital for the life of Israel for ages until the perfect sacrifice that Christ makes on the cross. For now, consider the specificity of God's demands for His people as a picture of divine holiness.

Selected Reading:
Hebrews 9:1-15 for a comparison of the Old Testament sacrificial system, epitomized by the Ark of the Covenant, with the sacrifice of Christ on the cross. The New Testament asserts that Jesus' blood remains so much more effective than the blood of goats and sheep in atoning for his people's sins.

Facts to Know

Ark of the Covenant	gold chest which held the Law and Ten Commandments
mercy seat	gold covering for Ark of the Covenant, with angels at each end; the "seat" or throne of the invisible God of the Hebrews
Tabernacle	tent which served as a portable sanctuary
table of showbread	every Sabbath, 12 loaves of sacred bread were placed on this table for the priests to eat
ephod	embroidered priestly vestment
menorah	the golden 7-branch lampstand

Memory Verse

Exodus 31:18

And he gave unto Moses upon Mount Sinai two tablets of stone, written with the finger of God.

The Tabernacle

68

Vocabulary and Expressions

1. **Ark of the Covenant, Ark of the Testimony**: can be used interchangeably for the ceremonial chest that was at the center of Israel's worship
2. **menorah**: the golden lampstand that had <u>seven</u> branches and burned oil. (The <u>nine</u>-branch Hanukkah candlestand is also called a menorah. Hanukkah celebrates the rededication of the Temple after the successful Jewish revolt against the Seleucid monarchy. According to the Talmud, the victorious Jews only had enough oil to light the menorah for one day, but the lamp miraculously burned for eight days until a new supply arrived.)
3. **sanctuary**: a sacred place set aside for worship

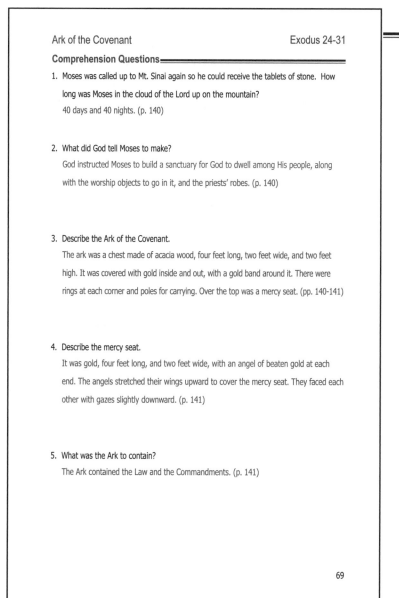

Ark of the Covenant   Exodus 24-31

Comprehension Questions

1. Moses was called up to Mt. Sinai again so he could receive the tablets of stone. How long was Moses in the cloud of the Lord up on the mountain?
   40 days and 40 nights. (p. 140)

2. What did God tell Moses to make?
   God instructed Moses to build a sanctuary for God to dwell among His people, along with the worship objects to go in it, and the priests' robes. (p. 140)

3. Describe the Ark of the Covenant.
   The ark was a chest made of acacia wood, four feet long, two feet wide, and two feet high. It was covered with gold inside and out, with a gold band around it. There were rings at each corner and poles for carrying. Over the top was a mercy seat. (pp. 140-141)

4. Describe the mercy seat.
   It was gold, four feet long, and two feet wide, with an angel of beaten gold at each end. The angels stretched their wings upward to cover the mercy seat. They faced each other with gazes slightly downward. (p. 141)

5. What was the Ark to contain?
   The Ark contained the Law and the Commandments. (p. 141)

69

Continue to recite the Books of the Old Testament and add the last four minor prophets.

- Hosea
- Joel
- Amos
- Obadiah
- Jonah
- Micah
- Nahum
- Habakkuk
- **Zephaniah**
- **Haggai**
- **Zechariah**
- **Malachi**

Activities

Pp. 138-139   What is happening in this picture?
Moses writes down all the words of the Lord that he has received at the top of Mt. Sinai. He then rises early in the morning and builds an altar to the Lord with twelve pillars for the twelve tribes of Israel, and he sacrifices an animal to God.

Pp. 140   What is this? The Ark of the Covenant with the mercy seat on top.

Pp. 141   What is this? The table of showbread with the golden lampstand.

What is the significance of the robes prepared for Aaron?
The special garments for priests show how important their ministry for the people is. They are consecrated or set apart for a special service to God.

Inside cover of GCB:
Find the Ark of the Covenant, the menorah, the Ten Commandments, a locust, and a frog.
What other pictures can you identify?

Review Lesson: Unit 4

Instructions

Use this Review Lesson to support mastery of the material presented in the previous five lessons. Drill the Facts to Know orally or have a Facts to Know Bee. Places to Know should be identified on the maps in this lesson. Events to Know will be reviewed in the timeline exercise which follows. Students may work independently on these two pages of the Review, but answers should be checked in class. A test for this unit is included in the back of this book.

Additional Review Materials: Discussion Questions

1. What did the Israelites do every time there was a problem?
   They would murmur and begin to wish they were still in Egypt.

2. Name as many examples of the Israelites' complaints as you can from the last four lessons.
   They complained about the water at Marah, food in the Wilderness of Zin, and water at Massah.

3. Draw and label all of the important locations of the Exodus journey to Sinai:
   - *Pithom*
   - *Red Sea*
   - *Marah*
   - *Elim*
   - *Rephidim*
   - *Mt. Sinai*

4. Draw and label the Tabernacle, with the Ark of the Covenant, the mercy seat, and the table of showbread with a menorah.

Review Lesson: Unit 4 (Lessons 16-20)

Events to Know in Salvation History
The Passover
Crossing the Red Sea
Bitter Waters Made Sweet
Manna From Heaven
Water From a Rock
Israel Defeats Amalek
Some Good Advice
The Ten Commandments
First Priest for Israel

People to Know
Moses
Miriam
Amalek
Joshua
Jethro
Aaron

Places to Know
Midian
Goshen
Mt. Sinai
Sinai Peninsula
Red Sea
Gulf of Suez
Gulf of Aqaba
Elim
Marah
Rephidim

Words to Know
Ark of the Covenant: golden chest containing tablets of Law and Commandments
mercy seat: golden cover of Ark, with angels at each end; throne of God
Tabernacle: portable tent sanctuary
table of showbread: held sacred bread in Tabernacle
menorah: 7-branch lampstand in Tabernacle
ephod: embroidered vestment
unleavened bread: bread without yeast
manna: bread from heaven
timbrel: musical instrument like a tambourine without parchment
omer: one-tenth a bushel of bread

Books of the O.T.
5-12-5-5-12

Law
Genesis
Exodus
Leviticus
Numbers
Deuteronomy

History
Joshua
Judges
Ruth
I II Samuel
I II Kings
I II Chronicles
Ezra
Nehemiah
Esther

Wisdom
Job
Psalms
Proverbs
Ecclesiastes
Song of Solomon

Major Prophets
Isaiah
Jeremiah
Lamentations
Ezekiel
Daniel

Minor Prophets
Hosea
Joel
Amos
Obadiah
Jonah
Micah
Nahum
Habakkuk
Zephaniah
Haggai
Zechariah
Malachi

70

Review Lesson: Unit 4 (Lessons 16-20)

Give the corresponding word or phrase:

1. The place of bitter waters in the Wilderness of Shur ____Marah____
2. Where God told Moses to strike the rock for water____Massah____
3. The golden chest that held the Law and Commandments _Ark of the Covenant_
4. Feast celebrating the Exodus from Egypt ____Passover____
5. The body of water east of the Sinai Peninsula ____Gulf of Aqaba____
6. The body of water west of the Sinai Peninsula ____Gulf of Suez____
7. Moses' father-in-law ____Jethro____
8. What tribe did the Israelite priests come from? ____Levi____
9. Number of days Moses was on Mt. Sinai ____40 days____
10. Bread without yeast ____unleavened bread____
11. Day of rest ____Sabbath____
12. Bread that rained from heaven in the desert ____manna____
13. The throne of pure gold on top of the Ark of the Covenant ____mercy seat____
14. What Israel ate with their lamb for the Passover __unleavened bread and bitter herbs__
15. What did the children of Israel always do when difficulties arose? ____murmur____
16. What great miracle did God perform in the Exodus? ____parting of Red Sea____
17. God gave the Law and Ten Commandments on this mountain __Mt. Sinai__
18. What figures were at either end of the mercy seat? _golden angels with wings outspread_
19. The 7-branch golden lampstand in the Tabernacle ____menorah____
20. The tent which served as a portable sanctuary for Israel ____Tabernacle____
21. The Israelites defeated these people on the way to Mt. Sinai __Amalekites__
22. Who defeated the Amalekites when Moses held up his hands? _Joshua_
23. He spoke with God directly ____Moses____
24. The 12 loaves of bread placed in the Tabernacle each Sabbath ____showbread____

List the Ten Plagues in order:

1. The plague of water and blood
2. The plague of frogs
3. The plague of lice
4. The plague of flies
5. The plague of cattle
6. The plague of sores
7. The plague of hail and fire
8. The plague of locusts
9. The plague of darkness
10. The death of the firstborn

71

Review Lesson: Unit 4

Old Testament Drill Questions

All of the short answer review questions from each Review Lesson have been compiled in Appendix 2. Continue to review them throughout the year. They are great for bees and competitions.

Additional Review Material:

List the ten plagues in order:

1. The plague of water and blood
2. The plague of frogs
3. The plague of lice
4. The plague of flies
5. The plague of cattle
6. The plague of sores
7. The plague of hail and fire
8. The plague of locusts
9. The plague of darkness
10. The death of the firstborn

Review Lesson: Unit 4

Timeline Review

Elementary-age children do not have a well-developed sense of time, especially time long ago and time over a long period. Putting events and people in order is also an advanced skill. These timelines are designed to teach beginning skills in creating a mental timeline of history. Students cannot do this work independently; this is a teacher-directed learning activity. Review the names Prehistory, Patriarchs, and Exodus, and the dates and people belonging to those periods. Next, go to "The Exodus and Wilderness Wanderings," number the events in order, and then complete the timeline.

Review Lesson: Unit 4 (Lessons 16-20)

Salvation History Timeline

The events of Salvation History are out of order! Number them in correct order. Then match people from the Review Lesson with events. Some people may be used more than once and in different combinations than shown in the list. Add the first two periods of Salvation History and their dates. You can find them in previous Review Lessons.

The Exodus and Wilderness Wanderings

_4_ Manna From Heaven	_7_ Good Advice
_2_ Crossing the Red Sea	_5_ Water From the Rock
_1_ The Passover	_3_ Bitter Waters Made Sweet
_6_ Israel Defeats Amalek	_8_ Ten Commandments
_9_ First Priest for Israel	

People
Moses
Miriam
Amalek
Joshua
Jethro
Aaron

Date	Events	Period	People
Time Begins		Prehistory	
2000 BC		Patriarchs	
1400 BC		Exodus cont.	
	Passover		
	Crossing the Red Sea		
	Bitter Waters Made Sweet		
	Manna From Heaven		Moses, Aaron, Miriam
	Water From the Rock		
	Israel Defeats Amalek		Joshua, Moses, Amalek
	Good Advice		Jethro
	The Ten Commandments		Moses
	First Priest for Israel		Aaron

72

Memory Verses

To recite memory verses, give the first few words and let students complete the verse orally. Students may write the verse from memory, from dictation, or copy it.

Review Lesson: Unit 4 (Lessons 16-20)

Scripture Memorization

Check each box if you can recite the Scripture verse from memory. Write each from memory or teacher dictation. Be accurate.

☐ **Exodus 12:13** _____

And when I see the blood, I will pass over you, and the plague shall not be upon you,

when I smite the land of Egypt.

☐ **Exodus 15:1** _____

Then sang Moses and the children of Israel:

   I will sing unto the Lord / For he hath triumphed gloriously

   The horse and his rider / Hath he thrown into the sea.

☐ **Exodus 16:4** _____

Then the Lord said to Moses, Behold I will rain bread from heaven for you.

☐ **Exodus 20:1-17** I am the Lord thy God, which have brought thee out of the land

of Egypt, out of the house of bondage.

   Thou shalt have no other gods before Me.

   Thou shalt not make unto thee any graven image.

   Thou shalt not take the name of the Lord thy God in vain.

   Remember the Sabbath, to keep it holy.

   Honor thy father and thy mother.

   Thou shalt not kill.

   Thou shalt not commit adultery.

   Thou shalt not steal.

   Thou shalt not bear false witness.

   Thou shalt not covet thy neighbor's wife, nor anything that is thy neighbor's.

☐ **Exodus 31:18**   And he gave unto Moses upon Mount Sinai two tablets of stone,

written with the finger of God.

73

Review Lesson: Unit 4

Memory Work: List the books of the Old Testament in order from memory.

The Books of the Law

1. Genesis
2. Exodus
3. Leviticus
4. Numbers
5. Deuteronomy

The Books of History

1. Joshua
2. Judges
3. Ruth
4. I Samuel
5. II Samuel
6. I Kings
7. II Kings
8. I Chronicles
9. II Chronicles
10. Ezra
11. Nehemiah
12. Esther

The Books of Wisdom

1. Job
2. Psalms
3. Proverbs
4. Ecclesiastes
5. Song of Solomon

The Books of the Major Prophets

1. Isaiah
2. Jeremiah
3. Lamentations
4. Ezekiel
5. Daniel

The Books of the Minor Prophets

1. Hosea
2. Joel
3. Amos
4. Obadiah
5. Jonah
6. Micah
7. Nahum
8. Habakkuk
9. Zephaniah
10. Haggai
11. Zechariah
12. Malachi

Review Lesson: Unit 4 (Lessons 16-20)

Timeline Review: Put the following in order on the timeline below.

1. **Dates:** Call of Abraham (2000 B.C.), Exodus (1400 B.C.)
2. **Periods:** Patriarchs, Exodus, Prehistory
3. **Events:** The Passover, A Baby Afloat on the Nile, The Creation, Twelve Sons, Twins Born to Struggle, The Ten Commandments, and The Child of Promise
4. **People:** Joseph, Noah, Moses, Seth, Adam, Jacob, Abraham, Isaac, and Joshua

Salvation History Timeline

Date	Events	Periods	People
		Prehistory	
	The Creation		Adam
			Seth
			Noah
2000 B.C.	Call of Abraham	Patriarchs	Abraham
	The Child of Promise		Isaac
	Twins Born		Jacob
	Twelve Sons		Joseph
1400 B.C.	A Baby Afloat	Exodus	Moses
	Passover		
			Joshua
	Ten Commandments		

75

More Timeline Review

We cannot overstate the importance of each student truly understanding the Old Testament chronology. The Bible is God's story and, as a story, sequence is very important!

We have included here a big picture practice timeline. Continue to help students identify the storyline based on the dates, periods, events, and important people.

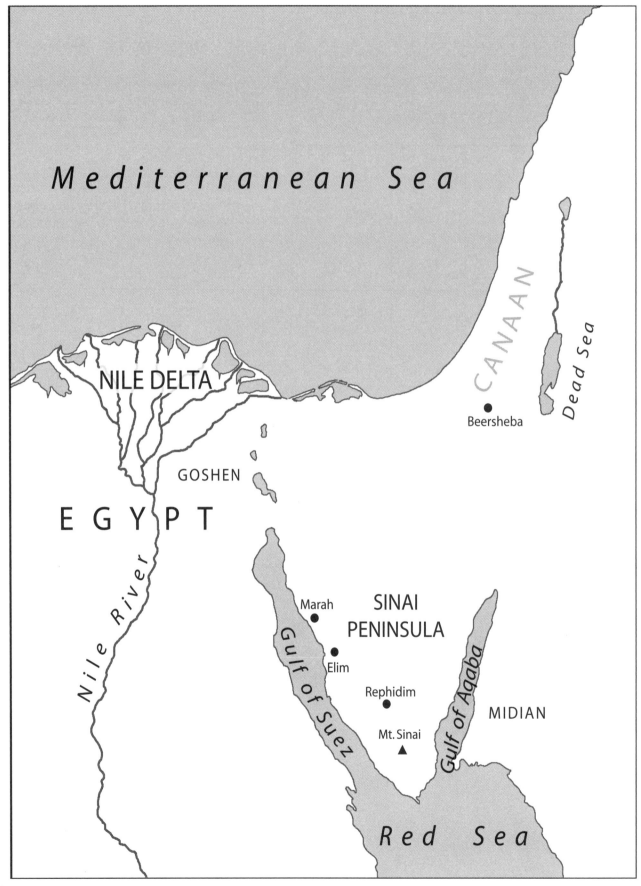

Mediterranean Sea

NILE DELTA

CANAAN

Dead Sea

Beersheba

GOSHEN

EGYPT

Nile River

Marah

Elim

SINAI PENINSULA

Rephidim

Gulf of Suez

Gulf of Aqaba

MIDIAN

Mt. Sinai
▲

Red Sea

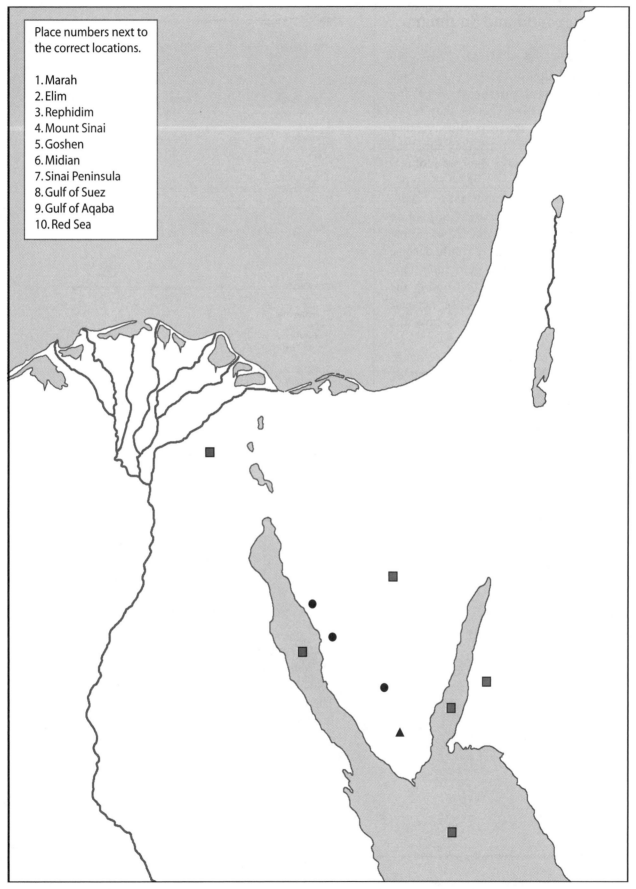

Place numbers next to
the correct locations.

1. Marah
2. Elim
3. Rephidim
4. Mount Sinai
5. Goshen
6. Midian
7. Sinai Peninsula
8. Gulf of Suez
9. Gulf of Aqaba
10. Red Sea

Lesson 21

Background and Summary

While Moses is on Mt. Sinai receiving God's revelation of the Law, the people grow impatient during this 40 day period. In their impatience, they revert to their old ways, the sort of lifestyle they practiced in Egypt. Thus, they enlist the help of Aaron to make them an idol that they can worship.

Here, it is vitally important to clarify that they intend to worship God, not an idol for a pagan god (Ex. 32:4). Some may wonder why the Lord would despise their actions if they had good intentions. Even though they want to worship the true God, their method is false, because revering a created image is how the pagans worshipped their false gods. Israel was forbidden to worship what pagans worshipped or how pagans worshipped.

Selected Reading:

I Corinthians 10:7-8 for Paul's warning to the church about the golden calf. In a cosmopolitan Greco-Roman city like Corinth, the church would be tempted with all sorts of pagan idolatry around them. Just like in Exodus, Paul makes it clear that idolatry is most often accompanied by other sorts of immorality.

Facts to Know

golden calf	the idol made by Aaron and the Israelites while Moses was on Mt. Sinai
proclamation	public announcement; from Latin "clamo"
engrave	to carve writing, figures, or designs into a solid material

Memory Verse

Exodus 32:9

And the Lord said unto Moses, I have seen this people, and behold, it is a stiff-necked people:

1. To what people is God referring?
   The Israelites

2. What does "stiff-necked" mean?
   stubborn

3. What does God mean by "I have seen this people"?
   He knows the faults of the children of Israel from experience.

78

Teacher Notes

1. Joshua apparently goes part of the way with Moses up the mountain, because he is not in the camp when the golden calf is made.
2. The Commandments are not written in stone by God's hand until the second trip up the mountain. At first, Moses receives them orally and writes them himself.

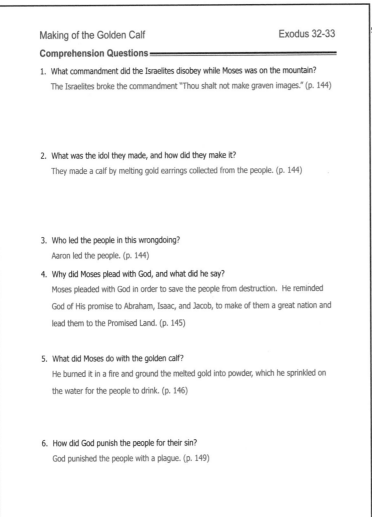

Making of the Golden Calf   Exodus 32-33

Comprehension Questions

1. What commandment did the Israelites disobey while Moses was on the mountain?

   The Israelites broke the commandment "Thou shalt not make graven images." (p. 144)

2. What was the idol they made, and how did they make it?

   They made a calf by melting gold earrings collected from the people. (p. 144)

3. Who led the people in this wrongdoing?

   Aaron led the people. (p. 144)

4. Why did Moses plead with God, and what did he say?

   Moses pleaded with God in order to save the people from destruction. He reminded God of His promise to Abraham, Isaac, and Jacob, to make of them a great nation and lead them to the Promised Land. (p. 145)

5. What did Moses do with the golden calf?

   He burned it in a fire and ground the melted gold into powder, which he sprinkled on the water for the people to drink. (p. 146)

6. How did God punish the people for their sin?

   God punished the people with a plague. (p. 149)

79

Continue to recite the Books of the Old Testament, working on mastering the minor prophets.

- Hosea
- Joel
- Amos
- Obadiah
- Jonah
- Micah
- Nahum
- Habakkuk
- Zephaniah
- Haggai
- Zechariah
- Malachi

Memory Work:

Review the Old Testament books of Law, History, Wisdom, the Major Prophets, and the Minor Prophets.

Activities

p. 145   What are the people doing? Can you find Aaron?
            The people are feasting and worshipping the golden calf. Aaron is standing on the far left of the picture.

pp. 146-147   Identify Moses. Why is he angry? What is he throwing?
              Moses is angry because the people are worshipping the golden calf. He is throwing the tablets of God at the base of the mountain and breaking them.

pp. 148-149   Identify Moses. What is Moses doing? Where is the golden calf?
              Moses is melting down the golden calf in the fire at the bottom of the picture. Moses ground the gold into powder and is sprinkling it on the water for the people to drink.

Lesson 22

Background and Summary

Disaster! Failure! Before Moses has even received the full revelation of the Law, the children of Israel have broken the second commandment by making the golden calf! Without Moses' prayers, the Lord might wipe Israel off the face of the earth! Does this mean that God's project of making a people for Himself is ruined?

By no means! Even from the earliest times, God's covenant with His people is based on His graciousness; just consider the promises given to Adam and Eve, Abraham, or Jacob. Even so, God grants restoration for Israel and renews His covenant with them, symbolized by making new tablets for Moses. Interestingly, at this time God reveals even more of Himself to Moses than He has previously (Ex. 34:4ff). For the people, He takes up His dwelling in the Tabernacle as a cloud by day and a pillar of fire by night (Ex. 40:34-38).

Unfortunately, the amazing mercy of God has yet to effectively change the obstinacy of the people. They continue to grumble and complain on the journey, but they will pay dearly for their next and greatest sin of unbelief at the borders of Canaan.

Selected Readings:

- **Deuteronomy 9** for Moses' account of how Israel provoked the Lord in the wilderness.
- **Deuteronomy 7:6-11** for Moses' paraphrase of what the Lord revealed of Himself on the mountain (Ex. 34:4ff). Here he tells Israel why God has been so faithful to them.
- **Psalm 67** for the psalmist's quotation of the memory verse and a great picture of how God would reveal Himself to the whole world through His blessing of Israel.

Facts to Know

Canaan	the Promised Land; a land flowing with milk and honey
House of Israel	Israelites
Wilderness of Paran	a desert three days' journey from Sinai
fleshpots of Egypt	expression describing the good food the children of Israel enjoyed in Egypt

Memory Verse

Numbers 6:24-26

The Lord bless you and keep you,
The Lord make his face shine upon you and be gracious unto you,
The Lord lift up his countenance upon you and give you peace.

1. What does it mean for the Lord to "make his face shine upon you"?
It means he gives you his blessing.

2. What is "countenance"?
Face; facial expression

3. How would one be gracious?
To be gracious would be to show compassion or favor.

80

Vocabulary and Expressions

1. **pomegranate**: a thick-skinned reddish fruit about the size of an orange with many seeds and a tart flavor. In Greek mythology, pomegranates are the food of the dead. (Bring examples of these to show the students.)
2. **fig**: an oblong or pear-shaped fruit common in the Middle East. (Bring examples to show the students.)
3. **"on this wise"**: in this manner
4. **"the sons of Aaron"**: the Levite priesthood

Twelve Spies Exodus 34,40; Numbers 10-13

Comprehension Questions

1. How long was Moses on the mountain with God when he rewrote the stone tablets?
   40 days and 40 nights. (p. 150)

2. What promise did God make to Israel?
   God promised He would drive out all the inhabitants of Canaan before them. (p. 150)

3. Where did Moses put the stone tablets?
   Moses put the tablets in the Ark of the Covenant in the Tabernacle. (p. 151)

4. What was over the Tabernacle by day and by night? How did the people know when to continue on their journey?
   The cloud of the Lord was over the Tabernacle by day and the pillar of fire by night. When the cloud lifted they could continue on their journey. (P. 151)

5. Why did the people murmur again?
   They complained about manna as their only food and recalled the better food they had in the land of Egypt. (p. 152)

6. What food did the Lord give them? How were they punished for their murmuring?
   God made a wind that blew large numbers of quail in from the sea, which the people ate. Then God sent a plague to punish the people, and large numbers of them died and were buried there. (p. 153)

7. Whom did Moses send into the land of Canaan, and why?
   Moses sent twelve spies, one from each tribe, to spy out the land. They were to see if the people of Canaan were strong or weak, few or many, if the land was rich or poor, if the cities had buildings or tents, and to bring back some fruit from the land. (p. 154)

8. Find on Unit 5 Map: ☐ Mt. Sinai ☐ Canaan ☐ Kadesh-Barnea

81

Teacher Notes

Read Numbers 6:22-23 before discussing the memory verse:
"And the Lord spake unto Moses saying, Speak unto Aaron and his sons saying, On this wise ye shall bless the children of Israel, saying unto them …"

These verses contain the priestly blessing for Israel. Notice the threefold repetition of the divine name, "the Lord" ("Yahweh" in the original text), which gives emphasis to the blessing. God Himself will bless the people with grace and peace through the Levite priesthood in very real ways.

Activities

p. 151   **What is Moses doing? What is behind him?**
Moses is on Mt. Sinai and has brought stone tablets for God to write on. Behind him is the cloud of the Lord.

pp. 152-153   **What is happening in the picture?**
The people are gathering quails that God had brought to the camp by a wind.

p. 154   **Identify pomegranates and grapes. What land is this?**
The pomegranates are in the tree, and the men are carrying huge grapes. The land of Canaan is in the background.

Draw the Tabernacle, Ark of the Covenant, and the cloud of the Lord over it.

Lesson 23

Background and Summary

In Numbers 13-14, Israel comes to a decisive moment in the short history of this budding people. Standing on the brink of entering the Promised Land, the people fail to trust the promise of God. Choosing to listen instead to the woeful warnings of the ten unbelieving spies, Israel commits its greatest sin against God in the wilderness. The next forty years testify to the seriousness of their offense.

Israel's lack of faith provides the center for understanding the whole message of Numbers: disbelief in Yahweh results in grave consequences. God determines that anyone age twenty or more will never see Israel take the Promised Land, but instead perish in the wilderness over the next forty years. During the time of their prolonged wandering, Israel continues to complain and evidence the fact that they were not ready to enter the land God had for them. Numbers contains episode after episode that display Israel's pattern of disbelief and disobedience.

In spite of Israel's continued sin, the Lord provides His means of restoration through the ministry of Moses and Aaron. Remember the healing brought by Moses' brass serpent on a staff and the refreshment of water from the rock at Meribah. These incidents picture the future salvation that comes in Christ, the great physician and the water of life. Even in the desert, God shows mercy and proves faithful to His promises.

Selected Readings:
- **Hebrews 3:12-19** for a warning through the example of Israel about the sin of disbelief that leads to apostasy.
- **John 3:14-16** for Jesus' words about how He will save God's people by being "lifted up" on a cross like Moses' brass serpent.
- **I Corinthians 10:4** for how the rock that gave water at Meribah foreshadows Jesus Christ, the source of living water.
- **I Corinthians 10:9-11** for a warning to the Corinthian church to avoid punishment like Israel received in the wilderness.

Lesson 23 (pp. 156-163)   The People Murmur

Facts to Know

Joshua and Caleb	two faithful spies
Eleazar	Aaron's son and successor
brass serpent	healed people of serpent bites
Edomites	tribe descended from Esau; refused passage to the Israelites
40 years	length of Wilderness Wanderings
"Gathered to his people"	expression that means to die, to go to be with his ancestors
Amorites	Israel defeated these people before the invasion of Canaan

Memory Verse

Numbers 14:2

And the children of Israel murmured against Moses and Aaron.

1. What does "murmured against" mean?
   It means they complained among themselves.

2. Why did the people murmur against Moses and Aaron?
   They feared having to do battle with the people living in the Promised Land.

82

Vocabulary and Expressions

1. **"land flowing with milk and honey"**: a phrase describing the plentiful resources of the Promised Land; sounds ideal when compared with 40 years in a desert wilderness
2. **"the sons of Anak, who was descended from giants"**: the Anakites were men feared for their great size and strength, part of the Nephilim, children of angels, and daughters of men (see Genesis 6:4)
3. **scapegoat**: a goat upon which the priest ceremonially placed the sins of the people and drove out of the camp

Wandering Continues   Numbers 13-14, 20-21

Comprehension Questions

1. What evil report did ten of the spies bring to Moses about Canaan? How did God punish them and the people for their lack of faith?

   The spies said the people of Canaan were too strong to overcome. The spies died of a plague, the murmurers died in the desert, and they did not enter the Promised Land. Even their children had to wander 40 more years before entering the Promised Land. (pp. 156-158)

2. Which two spies did not give an evil report about the land of Canaan? How did God reward them?

   Joshua and Caleb said they could take the land of Canaan because God was with them. They were able to enter the Promised Land. (p. 158)

3. In the Desert of Zin, when God told Moses to speak to the rock and water would come forth, what did Moses do? How did God punish him?

   Instead of speaking to the rock as instructed, Moses struck the rock. Moses also was not able to enter the Promised Land. (p. 159)

4. From whom were the Edomites descended? What did they do to the Israelites?

   The Edomites were descended from Esau. They would not give passage through their land, so the Israelites had to go around it. (p. 161)

5. Who became priest after Aaron and wore his priestly robes?

   The priest after Aaron was his son, Eleazar.

6. God sent serpents to bite the people when they murmured again. How did Moses make a remedy for the serpent bites?

   When the people looked at a brass serpent on a pole, they were healed.

7. What two tribes did the Israelites defeat and possess their land?

   The Israelites defeated the Amorites and the people of Bashan with their king, Og.

8. Find on Unit 5 Map: ☐ Edom ☐ Moab ☐ Mt. Hor

83

Teacher Notes

1. (Error in book on page 159. This should be the Wilderness of **Zin**, not Sin.)
2. In Genesis 19:30, 37-38, Lot's daughters bore him two sons, Moab and Benammi, the fathers of the Moabites and Ammonites, peoples that opposed the Israelites.

Activities

p. 156   What is happening?
            The people are murmuring against Moses.

p. 158   Who is the warrior?
            The warrior is an Amalekite, the tribe that struck down those who went on without Moses and the Ark of the Covenant.

p. 159   What is happening?
            Water is coming from the rock in the Desert of Zin after Moses strikes it.

pp. 160-161 What is happening?
            Aaron is requesting passage from the king of the Edomites. Moses and Aaron are climbing Mt. Hor where Aaron dies.

pp. 162-163 What people are fighting?
            The Israelites are defeating the Amorites.

Lesson 24

Background and Summary

As Israel draws closer to seizing the land of their inheritance, the Lord clears a way through all those that would oppose Israel or try to prevent the fulfillment of His promise.

The story of Balaam teaches us several things. First, we must recognize that in the Ancient Near East there lived other people such as Balaam who feared the one, true God as Israel did. Secondly, however, their faith in the true God was put to the test when they came in contact with the children of the promise, Israel. In this way, all those that would serve the true God must acknowledge the chosen people to whom He had revealed Himself.

When Balaam is tested, he nearly walks into the path of an angel. Before it is all over, though, Balaam recognizes the blessing of God on Israel and also announces that the future fulfillment of that blessing will come about in the day of Israel's king.

From this lesson, we should be warned to not walk through this life with spiritually blind eyes, but rather recognize and respond to God as He directs and guides us.

Selected Readings:

- **Genesis 49:8-10** for Jacob's prophecy of blessing that the scepter shall not depart from Judah.
- **Psalm 45:1-7** for a psalm about Israel's king who holds the scepter of God's righteousness. The king stands and rules for God and His ways.
- **Hebrews 1:8** for a quotation of Psalm 45:6-7 applied to Jesus as the Messianic King of God's people.

Lesson 24 (pp. 164-169)   Balaam and the King of Moab

Facts to Know

Balak	king of Moabites; asked Balaam to curse the Children of Israel
Balaam	a prophet from the north; Balak asked him to curse the Israelites
Moab	kingdom east of the Dead Sea; Lot was father of the Moabites
Balaam's ass	God opened its mouth to speak to Balaam

Memory Verse

Numbers 24:5,17

How goodly are your tents, O Jacob
And your Tabernacles, O Israel!
There shall come a star out of Jacob,
And a Scepter shall rise out of Israel

1. Who gave this blessing and prophecy? Balaam

2. What are the tents of Israel? the Tabernacles?
   The tents of the wandering Israelites were spread out in the valley below Balaam for shelter. The Tabernacle is the holy tent that contains the Ark of the Covenant, where God comes down to be with His people.

3. Who is Jacob? Israel?
   Jacob's name was changed to Israel. Both names refer to the Israelites, the children of Israel.

4. Who is the star that arises out of Jacob? King David

5. What is a scepter? Who is the Scepter that rises out of Israel? A scepter is the king's symbol of power. The Scepter is King David and his kingdom.

84

Vocabulary and Expressions

1. **goodly**: beautiful or lovely
2. **"more honorable"**: of greater authority and importance
3. **ass**: donkey
4. **scepter**: a staff held by a king as an emblem of authority
5. **prophesy**: *(verb)* to predict or announce the future or the will of God
6. **prophecy**: *(noun)* the words of a prophet, foretelling or predicting the future

Balaam and the King of Moab   Numbers 22-24

Comprehension Questions

1. Why did Balak fear the Israelites, and what did he ask Balaam to do?

   Balak feared the Israelites because he had heard of their victory over the Amorites and knew they were large in number. Balak asked Balaam to curse the Israelites. (p. 164)

2. What did Balaam's ass see that Balaam did not? How many times did Balaam beat his ass?

   Balaam's ass saw the angel of the Lord and would not go forward, so Balaam beat him three times. (p. 166)

3. What did Balaam instruct Balak to do?

   Balaam told Balak to build seven altars and prepare seven rams and seven oxen for sacrifice. The altars overlooked the valley where the Israelites were camped in their tents. (p. 168)

4. How many times did Balaam bless the Israelites?

   Balaam blessed the Israelites three times. (p. 168)

5. Why did Balak send Balaam back to his own land?

   Balaam blessed the Israelites, his enemies, instead of cursing them. (p. 169)

6. What prophecy did Balaam make before he left?

   Balaam prophesied that a great leader would arise out of Israel. He would conquer Moab and Edom and make the nation of Israel a great power. (p. 169)

7. Find on Unit 5 Map: ☐ Edom ☐ Midian ☐ Moab ☐ Dead Sea

85

Memory Verse

The first two lines of the memory verse are part of Balaam's blessing, and the second two lines are part of his prophecy about the future of Israel.

Hebrew poetry uses repetition a great deal. The first two lines contain the same praise, and the last two lines repeat the same prophecy.

Activities

pp. 164-165 Identify Balaam. Who is speaking to him?

Balaam is seated between his servants. The elders of Moab and Midian are asking him to come to Moab and curse the Israelites.

pp. 166-167 What is happening?

Balaam's ass sees the angel of the Lord, but Balaam and his servants do not. The ass crushes Balaam's foot against the wall when she will not go forward.

pp. 168-169 Describe this scene.

Balak has set up seven altars as Balaam has instructed, overlooking the tents of the Israelites in the valley. Balaam is blessing the children of Israel instead of cursing them.

Lesson 25

Background and Summary

The Israelites are posed on the edges of Canaan, about to enter the Promised Land. In spite of yet another scandal of covenant infidelity (Num. 25), the Lord has preserved a remnant of those that survived the Exodus as children to be His people in the land of their inheritance. Thus, Moses takes this opportunity to preach a series of sermons instructing the people how they should respond in this most decisive moment. These sermons compose the Old Testament book of Deuteronomy.

Aside from recounting the journey and cataloging the laws, the simple, consistent message of Deuteronomy is found in 4:9, which reads, "Only take heed to thyself, and keep thy soul diligently, lest thou forget the things which thine eyes have seen, and lest they depart from thy heart all the days of thy life: but teach them thy sons, and thy sons' sons." As you read the lesson, notice how many times you see the command to remember or not forget.

From Moses' sermon, we can apply three things: first, never forget what God has done for us in Christ; second, allow the memory of God's goodness to motivate the way we live each day; third, make that motivating memory the legacy of our families.

Selected Readings:
- **Joshua 24:15** for Joshua's paraphrase and restatement of the memory verse at the end of his life.
- **Matthew 4:1-11** for Jesus' testing in the wilderness before he began his earthly ministry. Note the most important similarities between the testing time Israel and Jesus, respectively, spent in the wilderness.

Facts to Know

Mount Nebo	where Moses died and was buried
Jordan River	flows from the Sea of Galilee to the Dead Sea; the Israelites crossed over it to enter the Promised Land
frontlet	small black case containing parchments with biblical passages, worn on the forehead and left arm during prayer

Memory Verse

Deuteronomy 30:19

I have set before you life and death, blessing and cursing; therefore choose life, that both thou and thy seed may live.

1. What are the two choices God set before the Israelites?
   The children of Israel could choose life and blessing, or death and curse.

2. How could the children of Israel choose life and blessing?
   By obeying the commandments of God, remembering what He had done for them, and remaining humble.

3. How could the children of Israel choose death and cursing?
   By disobeying the commandments of God, forgetting what He had done for them, and becoming proud.

4. What is "thy seed"?　"Seed" refers to offspring.

5. Whom did God call to witness this charge to the children of Israel?　God called Moses.

86

Vocabulary and Expressions

1. **"The Lord our God is one Lord"**: this phrase would be better rendered, "Yahweh is our God, Yahweh alone!"
2. **"the anger of the Lord be kindled"**: this means that God's anger is like a fire that grows stronger and brighter when Israel offends Him.
3. **blessing**: the physical goods and spiritual benefits that come from keeping God's covenant
4. **cursing**: the consequences of separation from the land and loss of blessing that comes when they break covenant
5. **"sleep with your fathers"**: in the Old Testament they believed that when someone left this life, they went to rest with their family in Sheol—the place of the dead

Death of Moses   Deuteronomy 6,8,28,30,32,34

Comprehension Questions

1. When the forty years of wanderings had come to an end, Moses gathered the people together and gave them his final words. Summarize what he said.

   Moses reminded the children of Israel of the commandments and laws God had given them, and also of the mighty signs and wonders He had performed in bringing them up out of the land of Egypt. He told them to teach these things to their children and to talk about them as they go about their daily lives so they would always be in their hearts. Moses told them that God had humbled them by making them dependent on Him, and to be wary lest they become proud when they have fine things in the Promised Land. Moses said they would be punished if they forsook the Lord. God has set before them two paths, obedience which leads to life, or disobedience which leads to death. They should choose life.

2. Who led the Israelites over the river Jordan into Canaan?

   Joshua (p. 174)

3. How old was Moses when he died, and where was he buried?

   Moses died on Mt. Nebo when he was 120 years old. He was buried in the land of Moab near Beth-Peor, but no one knows where. (p. 176)

4. What did God predict the Israelites would do?

   God predicted the Israelites would forsake the Lord and break their covenant with Him. (pp. 174-175)

5. Why was there no other prophet like Moses?

   No later prophet knew the Lord personally, face to face, like Moses, or performed such mighty signs and wonders as Moses did in Egypt. (p. 176)

6. Find on Unit 5 Map: ☐ Moab   ☐ Mt. Nebo   ☐ Jericho   ☐ Edom

          ☐ Jordan River   ☐ Dead Sea   ☐ Ammon

87

Teacher Notes

Israel spent 40 years in the desert, and Jesus spent 40 days in the wilderness. It rained 40 days in the Great Flood, and Moses was on Mt. Sinai for 40 days. The number 40 is associated with the idea of a transforming experience.

Activities

pp. 170-171   What is Moses telling his people? Who is beside him?

At the end of the forty years of wandering in the wilderness, and knowing that he will soon die, Moses is giving his people the commandments, statutes, and judgments they will need to live by in the land they are going to possess. Joshua is beside him.

pp. 174-175   Where is Moses? Why is he there?

Moses is on Mt. Nebo looking over into the Promised Land, which he will not enter. He dies on Mt. Nebo.

Review Lesson: Unit 5

Instructions

Use this Review Lesson to support mastery of the material presented in the previous five lessons. Drill the Facts to Know orally or have a Facts to Know Bee. Places to Know should be identified on the maps in this lesson. Events to Know will be reviewed in the timeline exercise which follows. Students may work independently on these two pages of the Review, but answers should be checked in class. A test for this unit is included in the back of this book.

Review Lesson: Unit 5 (Lessons 21-25)

Events to Know in Salvation History

The Exodus and Wilderness Wanderings
The Golden Calf
First Spies in Canaan
A Bad Report
The Priest's Son
Serpent Lifted Up
King Calls for a Curse
The Angel and the Ass
An Unexpected Blessing

People to Know
Moses
Aaron
Joshua
Caleb
Eleazar
Balak
Balaam

Words to Know
proclamation: public announcement
engrave: to carve writing, figures, or designs into a material
stiff-necked: stubborn
countenance: face
murmur: to complain
scepter: king's symbol of power
frontlet: small black case containing scriptures; worn on the forehead and left arm during prayer

Places to Know
Jericho
Kadesh-barnea
Canaan
Edom
Moab
Midian
Ammon
Mt. Sinai
Mt. Nebo
Dead Sea
Sea of Galilee
Jordan River

Books of the O.T.
5-12-5-5-12

Law
Genesis
Exodus
Leviticus
Numbers
Deuteronomy

History
Joshua
Judges
Ruth
I II Samuel
I II Kings
I II Chronicles
Ezra
Nehemiah
Esther

Wisdom
Job
Psalms
Proverbs
Ecclesiastes
Song of Solomon

Major Prophets
Isaiah
Jeremiah
Lamentations
Ezekiel
Daniel

Minor Prophets
Hosea
Joel
Amos
Obadiah
Jonah
Micah
Nahum
Habakkuk
Zephaniah
Haggai
Zechariah
Malachi

88

Review Lesson: Unit 5 (Lessons 21-25)

Give the corresponding word or phrase:

1. The Promised Land is called a land of ____ milk and honey ____
2. God caused him to give a blessing instead of a curse ____ Balaam ____
3. God sent fierce snakes to punish the children of Israel, but if they looked on this they would be healed ____ brass serpent on a pole ____
4. Israel defeated this people before entering the Promised Land ____ Amorites ____
5. Israel also defeated this king before entering the Promised Land ____ Og, King of Bashan ____
6. The two faithful spies ____ Joshua and Caleb ____
7. King of Moabites ____ Balak ____
8. The major river in the Holy Land ____ Jordan River ____
9. The descendants of Esau who refused to give passage to the Israelites ____ Edomites ____
10. Aaron's son ____ Eleazar ____
11. The children of Israel made this idol at Mt. Sinai ____ golden calf ____
12. Sacred object that went before the Israelites on their journeys ____ Ark of the Covenant ____
13. Who said, "There are giants in the land!"? ____ the faithless spies ____
14. Because of their sins, the Israelites wandered in the wilderness for ____ 40 years ____
15. Balak, the king of Moab, called upon this man to curse the Israelites ____ Balaam ____
16. The Moabites were descendants of Moab, the son of ____ Lot ____
17. It spoke to its master after being beaten three times ____ Balaam's ass ____
18. He died on Mt. Nebo without entering the Promised Land ____ Moses ____
19. Age of Moses when he died ____ 120 years ____
20. God told the children of Israel that ____ obedience ____ leads to life and ____ disobedience ____ leads to death. Choose life!

Match up the vocabulary words:

E proclamation — A. to complain
G engrave — B. face
F stiff-necked — C. king's symbol of power
B countenance — D. scripture encasing worn for prayer
A murmur — E. public announcement
C scepter — F. stubborn
D frontlet — G. to carve into a material

89

Old Testament Drill Questions

All of the short answer review questions from each Review Lesson have been compiled in Appendix 2. Continue to review them throughout the year. They are great for bees and competitions.

Review Lesson: Unit 5

Timeline

Review the names Prehistory, Patriarchs, and Exodus, and the dates and people belonging to those periods. Next, go to "The Wilderness Wanderings," number the events in order, and then complete the timeline.

Salvation History Timeline

The events of Salvation History are out of order! Number them in correct order. Then match people from the Review Lesson with events. Some people may be used more than once and in different combinations than shown in the list. Add the first two periods of Salvation History and their dates. You can find them in previous Review Lesson.

The Wilderness Wanderings		People
8	An Unexpected Blessing	Moses
2	First Spies in Canaan	Aaron
1	The Golden Calf	Joshua
3	A Bad Report	Caleb
6	King Calls for a Curse	Eleazar
5	Serpent Lifted Up	Balak
7	The Angel and the Ass	Balaam
4	The Priest's Son	

Date	Events	Period	People
Time Begins		Prehistory	
2000 B.C.		Patriarchs	
1400 B.C.		Exodus, Wilderness Wanderings	
	The Golden Calf		Aaron
	First Spies in Canaan		Joshua and Caleb
	A Bad Report		
	The Priest's Son		Eleazer
	Serpent Lifted Up		Moses
	Kings Calls for a Curse		Balak
	The Angel and the Ass		Balaam
	An Unexpected Blessing		

90

Memory Verses

To recite memory verses, give the first few words and let students complete the verse orally. Students may write the verse from memory, from dictation, or copy it.

Review Lesson: Unit 5 (Lessons 21-25)

Scripture Memorization

Check each box if you can recite the Scripture verse from memory. Write each from memory or teacher dictation. Be accurate.

☐ **Exodus 32:9** And the Lord said unto Moses, I have seen this people, and behold, it is a stiff-necked people.

☐ **Numbers 6:24-26**

The Lord bless you and keep you,

The Lord make his face shine upon you and be gracious unto you,

The Lord lift up his countenance upon you and give you peace.

☐ **Numbers 14:2**

And the children of Israel murmured against Moses and Aaron.

☐ **Numbers 24:5,17**

How goodly are your tents, O Jacob

And your Tabernacles, O Israel!

There shall come a star out of Jacob,

And a Scepter shall rise out of Israel

☐ **Deuteronomy 30:19**

I have set before you life and death, blessing and cursing; therefore choose life, that both thou and thy seed may live.

91

Review Lesson: Unit 5

Review Lesson: Unit 5 (Lessons 21-25)

The Books of the Law
1. Genesis
2. Exodus
3. Leviticus
4. Numbers
5. Deuteronomy

The Books of History
1. Joshua
2. Judges
3. Ruth
4. I Samuel
5. II Samuel
6. I Kings
7. II Kings
8. I Chronicles
9. II Chronicles
10. Ezra
11. Nehemiah
12. Esther

The Books of Wisdom
1. Job
2. Psalms
3. Proverbs
4. Ecclesiastes
5. Song of Solomon

Write the books of the Old Testament in order from memory:

The Books of the Major Prophets
1. Isaiah
2. Jeremiah
3. Lamentations
4. Ezekiel
5. Daniel

The Books of the Minor Prophets
1. Hosea
2. Joel
3. Amos
4. Obadiah
5. Jonah
6. Micah
7. Nahum
8. Habakkuk
9. Zephaniah
10. Haggai
11. Zechariah
12. Malachi

92

Review Lesson: Unit 5 (Lessons 21-25)

Timeline Review: Put the following in order on the timeline below.

1. **Dates:** Call of Abraham (2000 B.C.), Exodus (1400 B.C.)
2. **Periods:** Patriarchs, Exodus, Prehistory
3. **Events:** The Passover, A Name Change, Wilderness Wanderings, The Creation, The Sacrifice of Isaac, The Ten Commandments, and the Famine in Egypt
4. **People:** Joseph, Noah, Moses, Seth, Adam, Eve, Jacob, Abraham, Isaac, and Joshua

Salvation History Timeline

Date	Events	Periods	People
		Prehistory	
	The Creation		Adam & Eve
			Seth
	Fall of Man		Noah
	Noah's Ark		
	Tower of Babel		
2000 B.C.	Call of Abraham	Patriarchs	Abraham
	The Sacrifice of Isaac		Isaac
	A Name Change		Jacob
	Famine in Egypt		Joseph
1400 B.C.	Passover	Exodus	Moses
	Ten Commandments		
			Joshua
	Wilderness Wanderings		

93

More Timeline Review

We cannot overstate the importance of each student truly understanding the Old Testament chronology. The Bible is God's story and, as a story, sequence is very important!

We have included here a big picture practice timeline. Continue to help students identify the storyline based on the dates, periods, events, and important people.

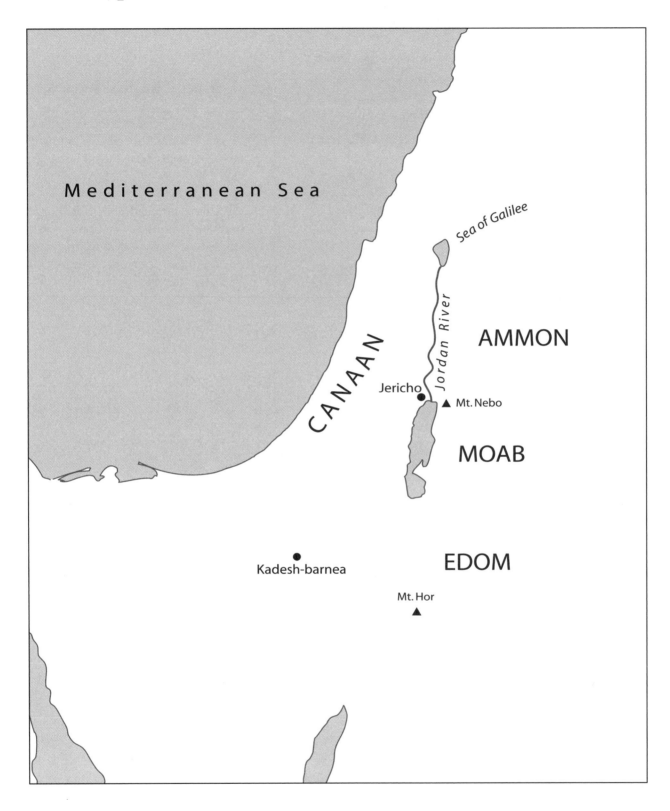

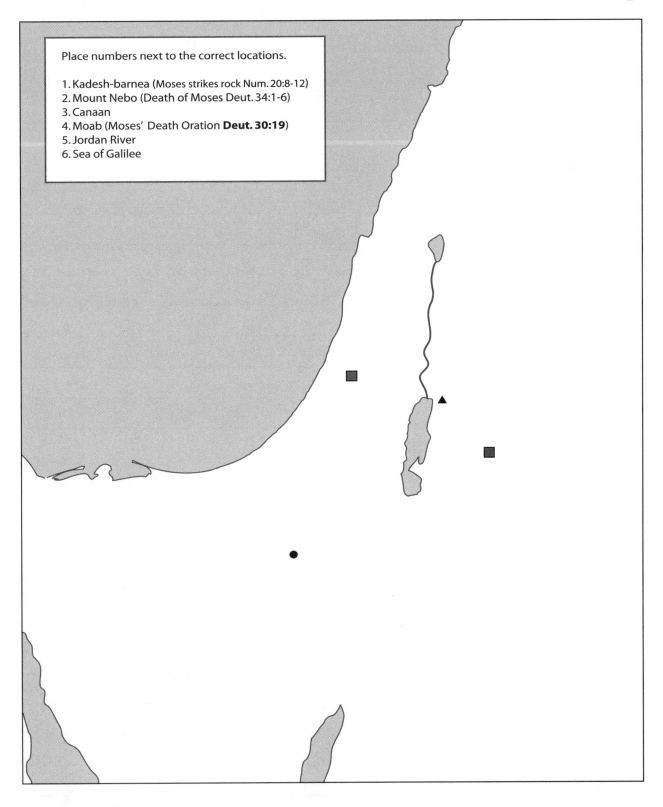

Place numbers next to the correct locations.

1. Kadesh-barnea (Moses strikes rock Num. 20:8-12)
2. Mount Nebo (Death of Moses Deut. 34:1-6)
3. Canaan
4. Moab (Moses' Death Oration **Deut. 30:19**)
5. Jordan River
6. Sea of Galilee

Christian Studies Final Review

Name: _____ Date: _____

Match the word or phrase to its definition. *(20 pts.)*

1. Place where God placed man to enjoy life *Garden of Eden* _____
2. Date of the call of Abraham _____ *2000 B.C.* _____
3. Father of many nations _____ *Abraham* _____
4. "He who laughs" _____ *Isaac* _____
5. The man who built the ark _____ *Noah* _____
6. Abraham's nephew _____ *Lot* _____
7. Abraham's wife _____ *Sarah* _____
8. Number of days and nights of the flood *40* _____
9. Wife of Isaac _____ *Rebekah* _____
10. Most cunning of the beasts _____ *serpent* _____
11. Symbol of God's covenant with man _____ *rainbow* _____
12. Tree that God forbid from Adam and Eve *Tree of Knowledge of Good and Evil* _____
13. Act of God making everything that exists _____ *Creation* _____
14. Where God confused language _____ *Tower of Babel* _____
15. Angels of God _____ *cherubim* _____
16. Age of Abraham when Isaac was born _____ *100* _____
17. Age of Sarah when Isaac was born _____ *90* _____
18. Adam and Eve's first sons _____ *Cain and Abel* _____
19. Bird that Noah sent out to find dry land _____ *dove* _____
20. A crisis caused by lack of food _____ *famine* _____
21. Jacob's beautiful wife _____ *Rachel* _____
22. Isaac's oldest son _____ *Esau* _____
23. King of Egypt _____ *Pharaoh* _____
24. Favorite son of Jacob _____ *Joseph* _____
25. Joseph's youngest brother _____ *Benjamin* _____
26. Isaac's son, received blessing _____ *Jacob* _____
27. Saved Joseph from death _____ *Reuben* _____

28. Jacob's plain wife _____ *Leah* _____

29. Held the 10 Commandments _____ *Ark of the Covenant* _____

30. Day of rest _____ *Sabbath* _____

31. Throne of pure gold _____ *mercy seat* _____

32. Bread without yeast _____ *unleavened bread* _____

33. Tent with an altar _____ *tabernacle* _____

34. Number of days Moses was in the mountains _____ *40* _____

35. One-tenth bushel of bread _____ *Omer* _____

36. Idol god the Hebrews made _____ *golden calf* _____

37. Bread provided by God _____ *manna* _____

38. Feast celebrating the Exodus of the Jews _____ *Passover* _____

Number the events of Creation in order

7	Sabbath, God rested
4	dry land, plants, trees
2	light and dark
3	sun, moon, and stars
6	land animals and humans
1	sky (separated the waters above from the waters below)
5	animals of the sea and sky

List the 10 plagues in order.

1. The plague of _____ *water and blood* _____

2. The plague of _____ *frogs* _____

3. The plague of _____ *lice* _____

4. The plague of _____ *flies* _____

5. The plague of _____ *cattle* _____

6. The plague of _____ *sores* _____

7. The plague of _____ *hail and fire* _____

8. The plague of _____ *locusts* _____

9. The plague of _____ *darkness* _____

10. The plague of _____ *death of the firstborn* _____

List the 10 Commandments in order:

1. Thou shalt _____ *have no other gods before Me* _____
2. Thou shalt not _____ *make any graven image* _____
3. Thou shalt not _____ *take the name of the Lord in vain* _____
4. Remember _____ *the Sabbath, to keep it holy* _____
5. Honor _____ *thy father and mother* _____
6. Thou shalt not _____ *kill* _____
7. Thou shalt not _____ *commit adultery* _____
8. Thou shalt not _____ *steal* _____
9. Thou shalt not _____ *bear false witness* _____
10. Thou shalt not _____ *covet thy neighbor's wife or belongings* _____

Answer the following questions with a phrase or sentence.

1. How did God make woman?

   From the rib of Adam

2. What was the only command God gave Adam in the Garden of Eden?

   Do not eat from the Tree of Knowledge of Good and Evil.

3. Who and what was to be let onto the ark?

   Noah, his wife, his sons and their wives, two of each kind of animal

4. Write the three promises God made to Abraham.

   1. He would have a son through Sarah.

   2. His descendants would be as numerous as the stars.

   3. He would inherit the land of Canaan.

5. Who found Moses in the river? What does his name mean?

   Pharaoh's daughter   drawn out

6. What does the Hebrew word Yahweh mean?

   "I AM" or "He who is"

7. How did the Israelites mark their homes so they were not victims of the last plague?

   They marked the top and side posts of their doorways with lamb's blood.

8. How old was Moses when he died?

   120

9. What was unique about Moses as a prophet?

   Moses spoke to the Lord face-to-face.

Fill in the missing books of the Old Testament.

Books of the Law:

1. *Genesis*
2. *Exodus*
3. *Leviticus*
4. *Numbers*
5. *Deuteronomy*

Books of History:

1. *Joshua*
2. *Judges*
3. *Ruth*
4. *I Samuel*
5. *II Samuel*
6. *I Kings*
7. *II Kings*
8. *I Chronicles*
9. *II Chronicles*
10. *Ezra*
11. *Nehemiah*
12. *Esther*

Books of Wisdom:

1. *Job*
2. *Psalms*
3. *Proverbs*
4. *Ecclesiastes*
5. *Song of Solomon*

Major Prophets:

1. *Isaiah*
2. *Jeremiah*
3. *Lamentations*
4. *Ezekiel*
5. *Daniel*

Minor Prophets:

1. *Hosea*
2. *Joel*
3. *Amos*
4. *Obadiah*
5. *Jonah*
6. *Micah*
7. *Nahum*
8. *Habakkuk*
9. *Zephaniah*
10. *Haggai*
11. *Zechariah*
12. *Malachi*

COPYBOOK VERSES

Do you remember these Copybook verses?

Old Testament

1. In the beginning God created the Heaven and the Earth. And the Earth was without form, and void; and darkness was upon the face of the deep. And the Spirit of God moved upon the face of the waters. And God said, "Let there be light!" and there was light. And God saw that the light was good: and God divided the light from the darkness. And God called the light Day, and the darkness he called Night. And the evening and the morning were the first day. Genesis 1:1-5

2. And God made two great lights, the greater light to rule the day and the lesser light to rule the night, and He made the stars also. Genesis 1:16

3. And God saw everything that He had made, and behold, it was very good. Genesis 1:31

4. And the Lord God formed man of the dust of the ground, and breathed into his nostrils the breath of life; and man became a living soul. Genesis 2:7

5. And the Lord God planted a garden eastward in Eden. Genesis 2:8

6. And the Lord God said, It is not good that man should be alone; I will make a help meet for him. Genesis 2:18

7. And Adam said, This is now bone of my bones and flesh of my flesh; she shall be called Woman because she was taken out of Man. Therefore shall a man leave his father and his mother, and shall cleave unto his wife; and they shall be one flesh. Genesis 2:23-24

8. Now the serpent was more subtle than any beast of the field. Genesis 3:1

9. And they heard the voice of the Lord God walking in the garden in the cool of the day. Genesis 3:7-8

10. And the woman said, The serpent beguiled me, and I did eat. Genesis 3:13

11. And Adam called his wife's name Eve, because she was the mother of all living. Genesis 3:20

12. Abel was a keeper of sheep, but Cain was a tiller of the ground. Genesis 4:2

13. Am I my brother's keeper? Genesis 4:9

14. But Noah found grace in the eyes of the Lord. Noah was a just man and perfect in his generation. Noah walked with God. And Noah begat three sons, Shem, Ham and Japheth. Genesis 6:8-10

15. Make thee an ark of gopher wood. Genesis 6:14

16. And the rain was upon the earth forty days and forty nights. Genesis 7:12

17. I do set my bow in the cloud, and it shall be for a token of a covenant between me and the earth. Genesis 9:13

18. Thy name shall be called Abraham, for a father of many nations have I made thee. Genesis 17:5

19. The voice is Jacob's voice, but the hands are the hands of Esau. Genesis 27:22

20. And they said one to another, Behold, this dreamer cometh! Genesis 37:19

21. They stripped Joseph out of his coat, his coat of many colors, and they cast him into a pit. Genesis 37:23

22. And she took for him an ark of bulrushes and daubed it with slime and with pitch. Exodus 2:3

23. Behold, the bush burned with fire, and the bush was not consumed. Exodus 3:2

24. I am the God of thy father, the God of Abraham, the God of Isaac, and the God of Jacob. And Moses hid his face; for he was afraid to look upon God. Exodus 3:6

25. A land flowing with milk and honey. Exodus 3:8

26. And Moses told Pharaoh, Let my people go! Exodus 5:1

27. Behold, I send an Angel before thee, to keep thee in the way. Exodus 23:20

28. Who is this uncircumcised Philistine that he should defy the armies of the living God? I Samuel 17:26

29. And David chose him five smooth stones. I Samuel 17:40

30. David, the son of Jesse, the anointed of God, the sweet psalmist of Israel. II Samuel 23:1

31. A soft answer turneth away wrath. Proverbs 15:1

32. A merry heart doeth good like medicine. Proverbs 17:22

33. A word fitly spoken is like apples of gold in pictures of silver. Proverbs 25:11

34. I am the rose of Sharon, the lily of the valleys. Song of Solomon 2:1

35. Behold, a virgin shall conceive and bear a son, and shall call his name Immanuel. Isaiah 7:14

36. The Lord is my shepherd; I shall not want, He maketh me to lie down in green pastures, He leadeth me beside the still waters, He restoreth my soul; He leadeth me in the paths of righteousness for His name's sake; Yea though I walk through the valley of the shadow of death, I will fear no evil, for thou art with me. Thy rod and thy staff, they comfort me. Thou preparest a table before me in the presence of mine enemies. Thou anointest my head with oil; my cup runneth over. Surely goodness and mercy shall follow me all the days of my life, and I will dwell in the house of the Lord forever. Psalm 23

37. Make a joyful noise unto the Lord, all ye lands. Serve the Lord with gladness; come before His presence with singing. Know ye that the Lord, He is God; it is He that hath made us, and not we ourselves; we are His people, and the sheep of His pasture. Enter into His gates with thanksgiving, and into His courts with praise; be thankful unto Him, and bless His name. For the Lord is good; His mercy is everlasting; and His truth endureth to all generations. Psalm 100

New Testament

38. Now when Jesus was born in Bethlehem of Judea in the days of Herod the king, behold, there came wise men from the east to Jerusalem saying, Where is he that is born king of the Jews? For we have seen his star in the east and are come to worship him. Matthew 2:1-2

39. And they saw the young child with Mary his mother, and they fell down and worshipped him. And when they had opened their treasures, they presented unto him gifts, gold and frankincense and myrrh. Matthew 2:11

40. You are the light of the world. A city that is set on a hill cannot be hid. Matthew 5:14

41. Our Father which art in Heaven, hallowed be Thy name. Thy kingdom come, Thy will be done, on Earth as it is in Heaven. Give us this day our daily bread, and forgive us our debts, as we forgive debtors. And lead us not into temptation, but deliver us from evil. For Thine is the kingdom and the power and the glory forever. Amen. Matthew 6:9-13

42. Ask, and it shall be given you; seek and ye shall find; knock and it shall be opened unto you. Matthew 7:7

43. By their fruits ye shall know them. Matthew 7:20

44. Many that are first shall be last; and the last shall be first. Matthew 19:30

45. For when I was hungry you gave me meat; I was thirsty and you gave me drink; I was a stranger and you took me in; naked and you clothed me; I was in prison and you came unto me. Matthew 25:35

46. Inasmuch as you have done it to the least of these my brethren, you have done it to me. Matthew 25:40

47. O my Father, if it be possible, let this cup pass from me; nevertheless, not my will, but thine be done. Matthew 26:39

48. Watch and pray, lest you enter into temptation. The spirit indeed is willing, but the flesh is weak. Matthew 26:40

49. Suffer the little children to come unto me and forbid them not, for of such is the kingdom of God. Mark 10:14

50. And she brought forth her firstborn son and wrapped him in swaddling clothes and laid him in a manger, because there was no room for them in the inn. Luke 2:7

51. There were in the same country shepherds abiding in the field, keeping watch over their flock by night. And lo, the angel of the Lord came upon them, and the glory of the Lord shone round about them, and they were sore afraid. And the angel said unto them, Fear not, for behold, I bring you good tidings of great joy, which shall be to all people. For unto you is born this day in the city of David a Savior, who is Christ the Lord. Luke 2:8-12

52. Glory to God in the highest and on earth peace, goodwill toward men. Luke 2:14

53. For God so loved the world that He gave His only begotten son. John 3:16

54. I am the bread of life. John 6:35

55. I am the good shepherd. The good shepherd gives his life for his sheep. John 10:11

56. I am the way, the truth, and the life. No man cometh unto the Father but by me. John 14:6

57. It is more blessed to give than to receive. Acts 20:35

58. The temple of God is holy, which temple ye are. I Corinthians 3:17

59. Behold, I stand at the door and knock. Revelation 3:20

60. I am the Alpha and the Omega, the beginning and the end, the first and the last. Revelation 22:13

OLD TESTAMENT DRILL QUESTIONS

Review Lesson 1

Give the corresponding word or phrase:

1. Latin for "image of God" _____ imago Dei
2. Adam and Eve's third son _____ Seth
3. Abraham's nephew _____ Lot
4. Most cunning of beasts _____ serpent
5. Where God placed man to enjoy life _____ Garden of Eden
6. He built the ark _____ Noah
7. Age of Sarah when Isaac was born _____ 90
8. Bird that Noah sent out to find dry land _____ dove
9. Where God confused language _____ Tower of Babel
10. Age of Abraham when Isaac was born _____ 100
11. Tree that God forbade to Adam and Eve _____ Tree of Knowledge of Good and Evil
12. In the Flood it rained this many days and nights _____ 40
13. Symbol of God's covenant with man _____ rainbow
14. Abraham's wife _____ Sarah
15. "He who laughs" _____ Isaac
16. Adam and Eve's first two sons _____ Cain and Abel
17. The act of bringing the universe into existence _____ Creation
18. An order of angels _____ cherubim
19. Date of the Call of Abraham _____ 2000 B.C.
20. Father of many nations _____ Abraham
21. She turned to a pillar of salt _____ Lot's wife
22. Two wicked cities destroyed by fire and brimstone _____ Sodom and Gomorrah
23. Sarah's handmaid, the mother of Ishmael _____ Hagar
24. "Out of nothing" _____ ex nihilo
25. Land given to Abraham as an inheritance _____ Canaan

Review Lesson 2

Give the corresponding word or phrase:

1. King of Egypt _____ Pharaoh
2. The three patriarchs _____ Abraham, Isaac, Jacob
3. The two sons of Jacob and Rachel _____ Joseph and Benjamin
4. Jacob's two wives _____ Leah and Rachel
5. Jacob's name was changed to _____ Israel
6. Isaac's twin sons _____ Jacob and Esau
7. Pharaoh's servants in prison with Joseph _____ butler and baker
8. She lied about Joseph _____ Potiphar's wife
9. Jacob's beautiful wife _____ Rachel
10. Egyptian who bought Joseph _____ Potiphar
11. Joseph's youngest brother _____ Benjamin
12. Joseph's two dreams _____ brothers' sheaves bowed to his sheaf; sun, moon, and stars bowed down to him

13. The three patriarch wives _____ Sarah, Rebekah, Rachel
14. Jacob's favorite son _____ Joseph
15. Jacob's dream_____ ladder with angels
16. He had a coat of many colors _____ Joseph
17. Joseph's two sons_____ Ephraim and Mannesseh
18. Number of years of plenty and famine _____ seven
19. Jacob's plain wife _____ Leah
20. Pharaoh's two dreams _____ lean and fat cows; blasted and fat ears
21. He sold his birthright for a mess of pottage _____ Esau

Review Lesson 3

Give the corresponding word or phrase:

1. Moses' sister_____ Miriam
2. Moses' brother _____ Aaron
3. Where Moses fled after killing an Egyptian_____ Midian
4. The Hebrew name for God _____ Yahweh
5. The part of Egypt Pharaoh gave to Joseph's family _____ Goshen
6. What does Yahweh mean? _____ "I am"
7. What was found in Benjamin's sack? _____ silver cup
8. He was hidden in a basket on the Nile _____ Moses
9. How did the angel of the Lord appear to Moses on Mt. Horeb? _____ a burning bush
10. Jacob prophesied this tribe would rule the others _____ Judah
11. The Nile empties into what sea? _____ Mediterranean
12. Which direction does the Nile flow? _____ south to north
13. What is the great river of Egypt? _____ Nile
14. The arc of land stretching from the Persian Gulf to Egypt _____ Fertile Crescent
15. Three names for God's people _____ Israel, Hebrews, Children of Israel
16. The children of Israel built these two cities for Pharaoh _____ Pithom and Ramses
17. The tribe of Moses and Aaron _____ Levi
18. The departure of Israel from Egypt in 1400 B.C. _____ Exodus

Review Lesson 4

Give the corresponding word or phrase:

1. The place of bitter waters in the Wilderness of Shur _____ Marah
2. Where God told Moses to strike the rock for water_____ Massah
3. The golden chest that held the Law and Commandments _____ Ark of the Covenant
4. Feast celebrating the Exodus from Egypt _____ Passover
5. The body of water east of the Sinai Peninsula _____ Gulf of Aqaba
6. The body of water west of the Sinai Peninsula _____ Gulf of Suez
7. Moses' father-in-law _____ Jethro
8. From which tribe did the Israelite priests come? _____ Levi
9. Number of days Moses was on Mt. Sinai _____ 40 days
10. Bread without yeast _____ unleavened bread

11. Day of rest _____ Sabbath
12. Bread that rained from heaven in the desert _____ manna
13. The throne of pure gold on top of the Ark of the Covenant _____ mercy seat
14. What Israel ate with their lamb for the Passover _____ unleavened bread and bitter herbs
15. What did the children of Israel always do when difficulties arose? _____ murmur
16. What great miracle did God perform in the Exodus? _____ parting of Red Sea
17. God gave the Law and Ten Commandments on this mountain _____ Mt. Sinai
18. What figures were at either end of the mercy seat? golden angels with wings outspread
19. The 7-branch golden lampstand in the Tabernacle _____ menorah
20. The tent which served as a portable sanctuary for Israel _____ Tabernacle
21. The Israelites defeated these people on the way to Mt. Sinai _____ Amalekites
22. Who defeated the Amalekites when Moses held up his hands? _____ Joshua
23. He spoke with God face to face _____ Moses
24. The twelve sacred loaves placed in the Tabernacle each Sabbath _____ showbread

Review Lesson 5
Give the corresponding word or phrase:

1. Idol made by the children of Israel while Moses was on Mt. Sinai ___ golden calf ___
2. The Promised Land is called a land of _____ milk and honey
3. God caused him to give a blessing instead of a curse _____ Balaam
4. God sent fierce snakes to punish the children of Israel, but if they looked on this they would be healed _____ brass serpent on a pole
5. Israel defeated this people before entering the Promised Land ___ Amorites
6. Israel also defeated this king before entering the Promised Land Og, King of Bashan
7. The two faithful spies _____ Joshua and Caleb
8. King of Moabites _____ Balak
9. The major river in the Holy Land _____ Jordan River
10. The descendants of Esau who refused to give passage to the Israelites Edomites
11. Aaron's son _____ Eleazar
12. The children of Israel made this idol at Mt. Sinai _____ golden calf
13. Sacred object that went before the Israelites on their journeys ___ Ark of the Covenant
14. Who said, "There are giants in the land!"? _____ the faithless spies
15. Because of their sins, the Israelites wandered in the wilderness for ___ 40 years
16. Balak, the king of Moab, called upon this man to curse the Israelites ___ Balaam
17. The Moabites were descendants of Moab, the son of _____ Lot
18. It spoke to its master after being beaten three times _____ Balaam's ass
19. He died on Mt. Nebo without entering the Promised Land ___ Moses
20. Age of Moses when he died _____ 120 years
21. God told the children of Israel that ___ obedience ___ leads to life and ___ disobedience ___ leads to death. Choose life!

106

WHO SAID THAT?

For each expression, identify the person or persons speaking.

1. "Take your shoes off your feet, for the place on which you are standing is holy ground."
   _____God_____

2. "Behold, the dreamer cometh." _____Joseph's brothers_____

3. "I have heard your voice in the garden ... I was afraid, and I hid myself." _Adam_

4. "Who is the Lord, that I should obey his voice?" _____Pharaoh_____

5. "Behold the fire and the wood: but where is the lamb?" _____Isaac_____

6. "And a scepter shall rise out of Israel." _____Balaam_____

7. "Hear, O Israel, the Lord our God is one." _____Moses_____

8. "Do not interpretations belong to God?" _____Joseph_____

9. "Am I my brother's keeper?" _____Cain_____

10. "Why did Sarah laugh? Is there anything the Lord cannot do?" _the Three Angels_

11. "Deliver me, I pray you, O God, from the hands of my brother." _Jacob_

12. "I do set my bow in the cloud." _____God_____

13. "Let us go at once and take possession of the land, for we are strong enough to
    overcome it." _____Caleb_____

14. "Let us make a name for ourselves lest we be scattered abroad on the face of the
    whole earth." _____the men of Babel_____

15. "It would have been better for us to have died in Egypt." _the murmuring Israelites_

16. "Behold the Lamb of God who takes away the sins of the world." _John the Baptist_

17. "Will you indeed destroy the righteous with the wicked?" _____Abraham_____

18. "I am that I am." _____God and Jesus_____

19. "God will provide a lamb." _____Abraham_____

20. "Therefore, choose life, that both thou and thy seed may live." _____Moses_____

21. "Then I cast it into the fire, and there came out this calf." _____Aaron_____

22. "Carry my bones up from hence." _____Joseph_____

VOCABULARY REVIEW

Match up the Words to Know with the definition:

S___ dominion

X___ cunning

AA___ enmity

W___ kindred

Z___ cleave

P___ score

U___ burnt offering

L___ famine

II___ kine

O___ birthright

Q___ firstborn

H___ venison

BB___ butler

M___ sackcloth

GG___ savory

EE___ sheaf, sheaves

HH___ plague

FF___ embalm

DD___ caravan

R___ midwife

CC___ yearn

C___ enchantment

D___ covenant

E___ timbrel

JJ___ omer

G___ imago Dei

B___ cherubim

A___ ephod

Y___ Yahweh

J___ ex nihilo

T___ engrave

K___ stiff-necked

N___ countenance

F___ murmur

V___ scepter

I___ frontlet

A. embroidered vestment

B. an order of angels

C. magic spell

D. a promise

E. musical instrument like a tambourine

F. to complain

G. Latin for "image of God"

H. meat from a deer

I. scripture encasing worn for prayer

J. Latin for "out of nothing"

K. stubborn

L. a lack of food due to crop failure

M. garment worn for mourning

N. face

O. family inheritance for the firstborn

P. twenty years

Q. heir of blessing

R. a woman who delivers babies

S. power or rule

T. to carve into a material

U. an animal burned as a sacrifice to God

V. king's symbol of power

W. relatives; tribe

X. crafty or sly

Y. "I am"

Z. to join or unite with

AA. hatred

BB. house servant

CC. to wish for or want

DD. a train of pack animals

EE. bundle(s) of wheat

FF. to preserve a dead body

GG. salty or flavorful

HH. widespread, destructive outbreak

II. cattle

JJ. one-tenth bushel of bread

More Timeline Review

We cannot overstate the importance of each student truly understanding the Old Testament chronology. The Bible composes God's story and, as a story primarily, sequence is everything!

We have included here a final big picture timeline. Continue to help students identify the story based on the dates, periods, events, and important people. In this way, the most significant components of the timeline will correspond with one another (Ex. 1400 B.C. = Exodus = Moses).

Given the consistent practice above, they should be able to recall the order in which these items fall, and sequence them appropriately.

OLD TESTAMENT TIMELINE

Appendix 5

Timeline Review: Put the following in order on the timeline below. Use each only once.

1. **Dates:** Time Begins, Exodus (1400 B.C.), and Call of Abraham (2000 B.C.)
2. **Periods:** Patriarchs, Exodus, Prehistory
3. **Events:** The Passover, A Name Change, The Golden Calf, The Fall of Man, Wilderness Wanderings, A Birthright Stolen, First Spies in Canaan, The Creation, Labor of Love, God Provides a Lamb, The Tower of Babel, The Ten Commandments, The Flood, The Burning Bush, The First Murder, The Famine in Egypt, Call of Abraham
4. **People:** Cain, Rachel, Joseph, Aaron, Noah, Abel, Moses, Esau, Adam, Caleb, Jacob, Eve, Abraham, Isaac, and Joshua

Date	Events	Periods	People
Time Begins	The Creation	Prehistory	
	The Fall of Man		Adam and Eve
	The First Murder		Cain and Abel
	The Flood		Noah
	The Tower of Babel		
2000 B.C.	Call of Abraham	Patriarchs	Abraham
	God Provides a Lamb		Isaac
	A Birthright Stolen		Jacob and Esau
	Labor of Love		Rachel
	A Name Change		
	The Famine in Egypt		Joseph
1400 B.C.	The Burning Bush	Exodus	Moses
	The Passover		
	The Ten Commandments		
	The Golden Calf		Aaron
	First Spies in Canaan		Joshua and Caleb
	Wilderness Wanderings		

OLD TESTAMENT TIMELINE

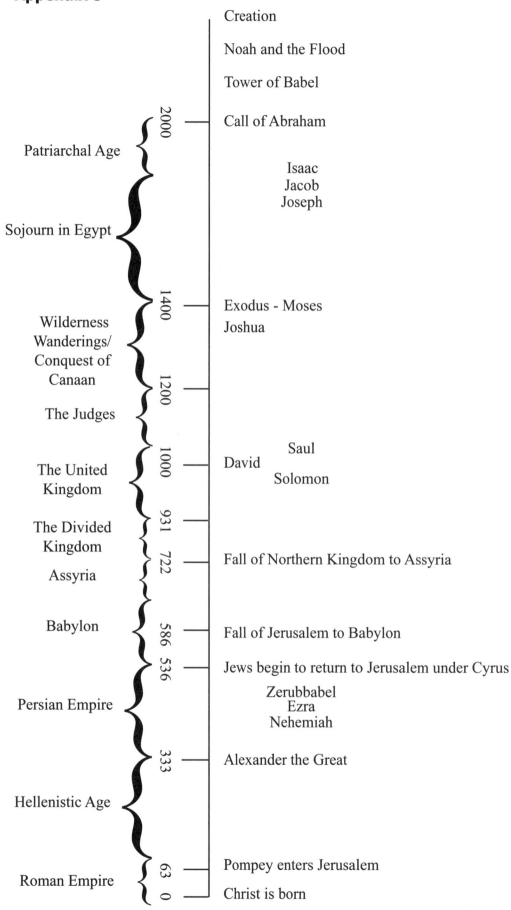

Creation

Noah and the Flood

Tower of Babel

Call of Abraham

Patriarchal Age

Isaac
Jacob
Joseph

Sojourn in Egypt

2000

Wilderness
Wanderings/
Conquest of
Canaan

1400
Exodus - Moses
Joshua

The Judges

1200

The United
Kingdom

1000
Saul
David
Solomon

The Divided
Kingdom

931

Assyria

722
Fall of Northern Kingdom to Assyria

Babylon

586
Fall of Jerusalem to Babylon

536
Jews begin to return to Jerusalem under Cyrus

Zerubbabel
Ezra
Nehemiah

Persian Empire

333
Alexander the Great

Hellenistic Age

Roman Empire

63
Pompey enters Jerusalem

0
Christ is born

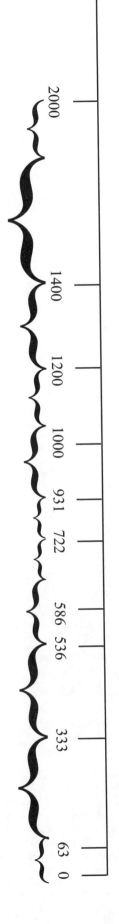

BOOKS OF THE OLD TESTAMENT

Law   5

Genesis	Book of Beginnings
Exodus	Deliverance from Egyptian Bondage
Leviticus	Book of the Law
Numbers	Wilderness Wanderings
Deuteronomy	Second Book of the Law

History   12

Joshua	Conquest of Canaan
Judges	No King in Israel
Ruth	The Great Grandmother of David
I II Samuel	Saul and David
I II Kings	Solomon and the Divided Kingdom
I II Chronicles	The Southern Kingdom of Judah
Ezra	The Jews Return to Jerusalem
Nehemiah	The Cupbearer of Xerxes Visits Jerusalem
Esther	A Jewish Queen in the Persian Court

Wisdom   5

Job	The Patience and Suffering of Job
Psalms	The Song Book of Israel
Proverbs	Wise Sayings for Daily Living
Ecclesiastes	All is Vanity
Song of Solomon	A Wedding Love Song

Major Prophets   5

Isaiah	A Prophet for Judah
Jeremiah	A Religion of the Heart
Lamentations	Laments for the Fall of Jerusalem
Ezekiel	Dry Bones
Daniel	Visions, Dreams, and Daniel in the Lion's Den

Minor Prophets   12

Prophets to Israel and Judah

Hosea	An unfaithful wife symbolizes unfaithful Israel
Joel	The Day of the Lord is coming for Judah
Amos	God requires justice and righteousness
Obadiah	God's judgment on Edom
Jonah	A mission to Nineveh and three days in a whale

Prophets to Judah

Micah	Judgment for Israel & Judah; future glory for little Bethlehem
Nahum	God's judgment on Nineveh
Habakkuk	God will use Babylon to punish the wickedness of Judah
Zephaniah	The Day of the Lord is coming for Judah and the nations

Postexilic Prophets

Haggai	A Call to Rebuild the Temple
Zechariah	Rebuild the Temple, the Messiah is coming
Malachi	A final warning, the Day of the Lord will come.

---

*Deuterocanonical Books   7

Tobit	Wisdom
Judith	Sirach
I Maccabees	Baruch
II Maccabees	

*The "deuterocanonical" books, most likely written in Aramaic, are included in Catholic and Eastern Orthodox Bibles. These books are found in historic Bibles such as the Greek Septuagint and the Latin Vulgate, and even though they are considered apocryphal (disputed) by Protestants, they are important documents for the study of Israel and the church; for this reason, students should learn them. Latin students will encounter the deuterocanon when they begin Latin translation with the Vulgate.

TEST I (85 total points) _____ Name

I.   Complete this memory verse: Genesis 12:1-3 (10 points)

Now the Lord said unto Abram, " _____

_____

_____

_____

II.   Matching. (10 points)

_____ 1. Adam and Eve's third son   a. Shem, Ham, Japheth

_____ 2. Land between the rivers   b. Garden of Eden

_____ 3. Sarah's handmaid; the mother of Ishmael   c. Sodom and Gomorrah

_____ 4. Two wicked cities; destroyed by fire and brimstone d. Hagar

_____ 5. Where God placed man to enjoy life   e. Ishmael

_____ 6. He who laughs   f. Seth

_____ 7. Mountain where Ark came to rest   g. Mesopotamia

_____ 8. Modern Mesopotamia   h. Ararat

_____ 9. Noah's sons   i. Isaac

_____ 10. Son of Abraham and Hagar   j. Iraq

III. Vocabulary. Choose the correct word from the word bank. (10 points)

cherubim	cunning	ex nihilo
cleave	dominion	imago Dei
covenant imago Dei	enmity	kindred
		sacred

1. image of God _____   6. clever; crafty_____

2. power; rule _____   7. to join or unite with _____

3. order of angels _____   8. out of nothing_____

4. relatives; tribe_____   9. snake_____

5. God's promise _____   10. ill will_____

IV.   Identification. (20 points)

1. Abraham's nephew_____

2. Abraham's wife _____

3. Land given to Abraham as an inheritance _____

4. Where God confused language _____

5. Date of Call of Abraham _____

6. Symbol of God's covenant with man _____

7. She turned to a pillar of salt _____

8. Adam and Eve's first two sons _____

9. Father of many nations _____

10. Sin of Adam and Eve _____

V. Answer in complete sentences. (3 points each: 9 points)

1. How did God make woman? _____

   _____

2. What work did Cain do? What work did Abel do? _____

   _____

3. How long did it rain? How long was the Great Flood upon the earth? _____

   _____

   _____

VI. Number the events of Salvation History in order. (6 points)

_____ First Murder

_____ The Creation

_____ The Flood

_____ Call of Abraham

_____ Fall of Man

_____ Tower of Babel

VII. Number the days of Creation. (7 points)

_____ animals and humans   _____ dry land, seas, plants

_____ sun, moon, stars   _____ Sabbath, day of rest

_____ animals of seas and air   _____ matter, light and dark, day and night

_____ sky; separated the waters

VIII. Map. Write the correct number next to its location on each map that follows. (23 points)

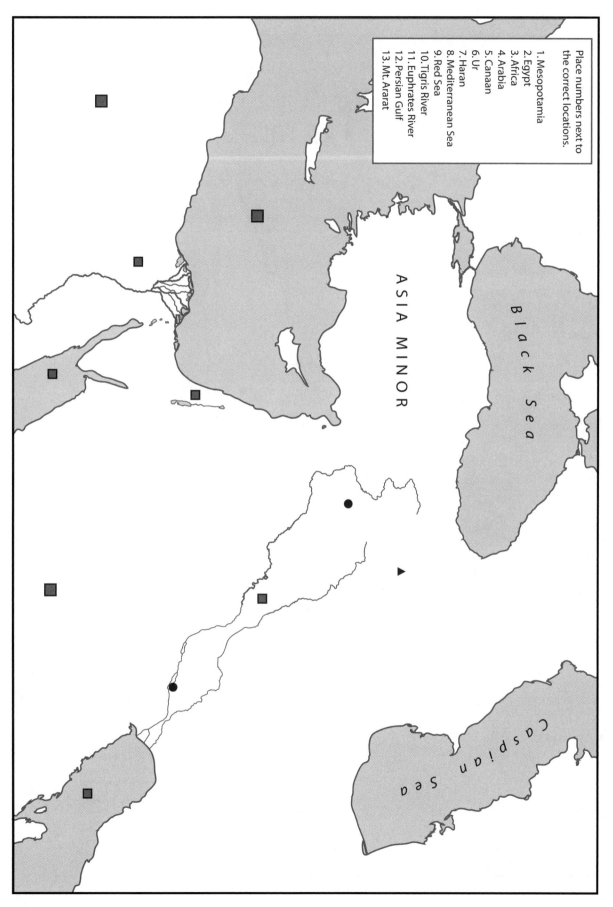

Place numbers next to
the correct locations.

1. Mesopotamia
2. Egypt
3. Africa
4. Arabia
5. Canaan
6. Ur
7. Haran
8. Mediterranean Sea
9. Red Sea
10. Tigris River
11. Euphrates River
12. Persian Gulf
13. Mt. Ararat

ASIA MINOR

Black Sea

Caspian Sea

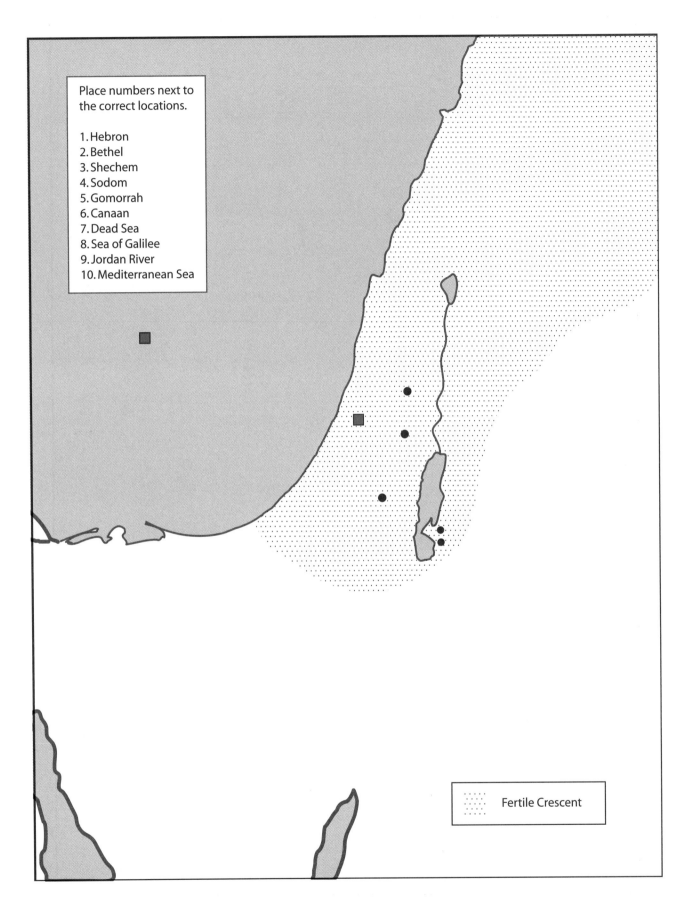

Place numbers next to
the correct locations.

1. Hebron
2. Bethel
3. Shechem
4. Sodom
5. Gomorrah
6. Canaan
7. Dead Sea
8. Sea of Galilee
9. Jordan River
10. Mediterranean Sea

Fertile Crescent

TEST II (84 total points) _____ Name

I.   Complete this memory verse: Genesis 22:7-8 (10 points)

And Isaac spake unto Abraham his father and said, " _____

_____

_____

_____

II.   Matching. (10 points)

_____1. Joseph's youngest brother   a. Ephraim, Manasseh

_____2. The two sons of Jacob and Rachel   b. Simeon

_____3. Rebekah's brother; father of Leah and Rachel   c. Leah

_____4. Jacob's plain wife   d. Joseph, Benjamin

_____5. Joseph's brother who was kept behind in Egypt   e. Reuben

_____6. She lied about Joseph   f. Laban

_____7. Jacob's beautiful wife   g. Potiphar

_____8. Joseph's oldest brother who saved him from death h. Potiphar's wife

_____9. Egyptian who bought Joseph   i. Rachel

_____10. Joseph's two sons   j. Benjamin

III.   Vocabulary. Choose the correct word from the word bank. (10 points)

burnt offering	kine	score
butler	sackcloth	sheaf
famine	savory	venison
firstborn		

1. male servant _____   6. salty; flavorful _____

2. bundle of wheat _____   7. twenty _____

3. cattle _____   8. deer meat _____

4. heir of blessing _____   9. mourning garment _____

5. sacrifice to God _____   10. complete lack of food _____

IV.   Identification. (10 points)

1. Jacob's favorite son _____

2. The three patriarchs _____

3. Sold birthright for a mess of pottage _____

4. The king of Egypt _____

117

5. Isaac's twin sons _____

6. The three patriarch wives _____

7. Jacob's name was changed to _____

8. He had a coat of many colors _____

9. Pharaoh's servants, in prison with Joseph _____

10. Number of years of plenty and famine _____

V.   Match the dreamer to the dream. (7 points)

_____1. seven full ears and seven blasted ears   a. Joseph (2)

_____2. your sheaves bowed down to my sheaf   b. baker

_____3. ladder reaching to Heaven   c. Pharaoh (2)

_____4. pressed grapes into Pharaoh's cup   d. butler

_____5. seven fat cows and seven thin cows   e. Jacob

_____6. birds ate from baskets of bread

_____7. sun, moon, and stars bowed down to me

VI.   Answer in complete sentences. (9 points)

1. Why did Esau sell his birthright? _____

_____

2. Why did Joseph's brothers plot against him? _____

_____

_____

3. What did the brothers find in their grain sacks on the way home? _____

_____

VII. Write the first 17 books of the Bible in order. (17 points)

Use the word bank for correct spelling.

1. _____   10. _____

2. _____   11. _____

3. _____   12. _____

4. _____   13. _____

5. _____   14. _____

6. _____   15. _____

7. _____   16. _____

8. _____   17. _____

9. _____

I Samuel	I Chronicles	II Kings	Ezra	Numbers
Genesis	Nehemiah	Joshua	Leviticus	
I Kings	II Samuel	Esther	Judges	
Exodus	Ruth	Deuteronomy	II Chronicles	

VIII. Map. Write the correct number next to its location on the map. (11 points)

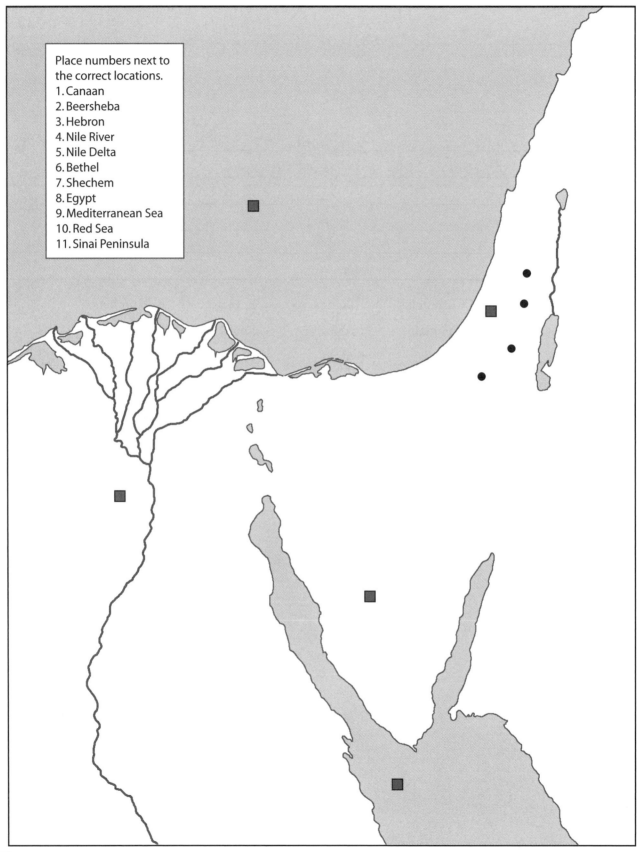

Place numbers next to the correct locations.
1. Canaan
2. Beersheba
3. Hebron
4. Nile River
5. Nile Delta
6. Bethel
7. Shechem
8. Egypt
9. Mediterranean Sea
10. Red Sea
11. Sinai Peninsula

TEST III (86 total points) _____ Name

I.   Complete this memory verse: Exodus 7:3 (5 points)

      And I will harden _____

      _____

II.   Matching. (10 points)

_____ 1. Moses' sister   a. Pharaoh's daughter

_____ 2. Burial plot of patriarchs and their wives   b. Judah

_____ 3. Jacob prophesied this tribe would rule the others   c. Pithom and Ramses

_____ 4. Arc of land from the Persian Gulf to Egypt   d. Miriam

_____ 5. Moses' brother   e. Goshen

_____ 6. Raised Moses as her own son   f. Field of Machpelah

_____ 7. Part of Egypt given by Pharaoh to Joseph's family   g. Levi

_____ 8. Tribe of Moses and Aaron   h. silver cup

_____ 9. Found in Benjamin's sack   i. Aaron

_____ 10. Cities built for Pharaoh by children of Israel   j. Fertile Crescent

III.   Vocabulary. Choose the correct word from the word bank. (10 points)

caravan	Eve	plague
embalm	Judah	Yahweh
enchantment	midwife	yearn
	Moses	

1. "I will praise" _____   6. to preserve a dead body _____

2. a destructive outbreak _____   7. mother of all living _____

3. to wish for _____   8. magic spell _____

4. "I am" _____   9. "drawn out" _____

5. a train of pack animals _____   10. delivers babies _____

IV.   Identification. (10 points)

1. Great river of Egypt _____

2. Where Moses fled after killing an Egyptian _____

3. Sea the Nile empties into _____

4. Departure of Israelites from Egypt _____

5. Direction in which the Nile flows _____

121

6. Hidden in a basket on the Nile _____

7. Meaning of "Yahweh" _____

8. How angel appeared to Moses on Mt. Horeb_____

9-10. Two names for God's people _____

V. Answer in complete sentences. (9 points)

1. What did Pharaoh order midwives to do to Hebrew sons? _____

_____

2. Why did Moses flee from Egypt to the land of Midian? _____

_____

3. What message did God send to Pharaoh through Moses and Aaron? _____

_____

VI. Number the events of Salvation History in order. (6 points)

_____ Exile in Midian _____ Ten Plagues

_____ Burning Bush _____ A Hard Heart

_____ Baby Afloat on the Nile _____ The Murderer Flees

TEST III

VII. Write the first 22 books of the Bible in order. (22 points)

Use the word bank for correct spelling.

1. _____   12. _____
2. _____   13. _____
3. _____   14. _____
4. _____   15. _____
5. _____   16. _____
6. _____   17. _____
7. _____   18. _____
8. _____   19. _____
9. _____   20. _____
10. _____   21. _____
11. _____   22. _____

I Samuel	II Samuel	Ezra	Song of Solomon
Genesis	Ruth	Leviticus	Proverbs
I Kings	II Kings	Judges	Ecclesiastes
Exodus	Joshua	II Chronicles	Job
I Chronicles	Esther	Numbers	
Nehemiah	Deuteronomy	Psalms	

VIII. Map. Write the correct number next to its location on the map. (14 points)

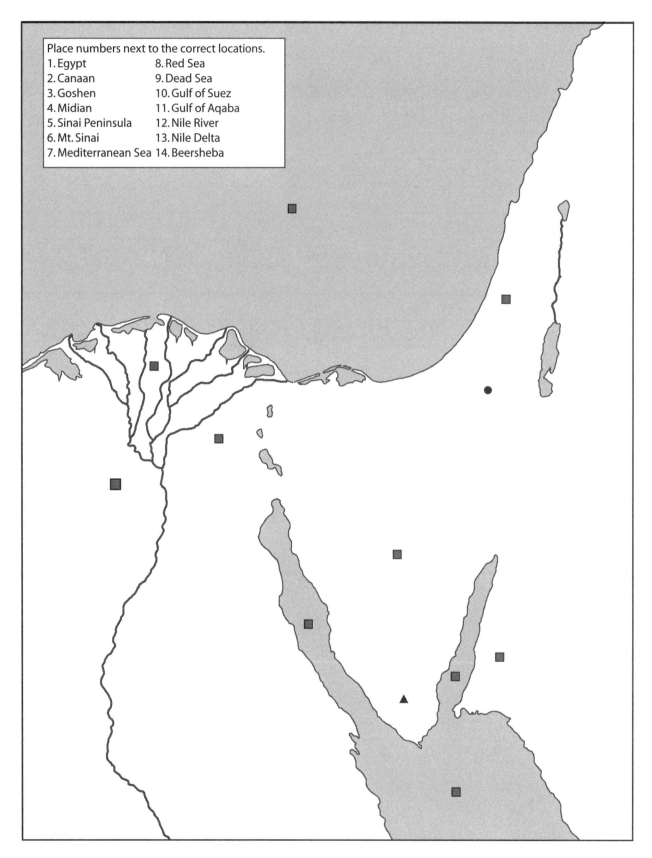

Place numbers next to the correct locations.
1. Egypt   8. Red Sea
2. Canaan   9. Dead Sea
3. Goshen   10. Gulf of Suez
4. Midian   11. Gulf of Aqaba
5. Sinai Peninsula   12. Nile River
6. Mt. Sinai   13. Nile Delta
7. Mediterranean Sea 14. Beersheba

TEST IV (92 total points)   _____ Name

I.   Complete this memory verse: Exodus 31:18 (5 points)

      And he gave unto Moses _____

      _____

II.   Matching. (10 points)

      _____1. Figures at either end of the mercy seat   a. showbread

      _____2. To strongly desire that which belongs to another b. mercy seat

      _____3. Held the Law and the Commandments   c. Jethro

      _____4. Golden throne on the Ark of the Covenant   d. menorah

      _____5. 7-branch lampstand in the Tabernacle   e. Marah

      _____6. To lie about someone   f. Amalekites

      _____7. Moses' father-in-law   g. Ark of the Covenant

      _____8. Bitter waters in the Wilderness of Shur   h. golden angels

      _____9. Bread placed in the Tabernacle each Sabbath   i. bear false witness

      _____10. Defeated by the Israelites on the way to Mt. Sinai j. covet

III. Number the items of the Tabernacle corresponding to names in the word bank. (8 points)

+---+
| 1. Altar of Incense   2. Lampstand |
| |
| 3. Most Holy Place   4. Laver |
| |
| 5. Ark of the Covenant   6. Altar of Burnt Offering |
| |
| 7. Table of Showbread   8. Holy Place |
+---+

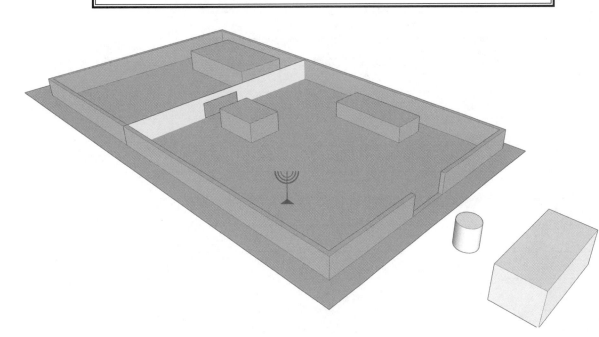

TEST IV

IV. Identification. (10 points)

1. Bread that rained from Heaven in the desert _____
2. He spoke directly with God _____
3. Feast celebrating the Exodus from Egypt _____
4. Number of days Moses was on Mt. Sinai_____
5. What the children of Israel always did when difficulties arose _____
6. Mountain where God gave the Law and the Commandments_____
7. Great miracle of the Exodus_____
8. Defeated the Amalekites when Moses raised his hands_____
9. Tribe the priests of Israel came from _____
10. Tent that served as a portable sanctuary_____

V. Write the Ten Commandments. (10 points)

1. _____

_____

2. _____

_____

3. _____

_____

4. _____

_____

5. _____

_____

6. _____

_____

7. _____

_____

8. _____

_____

9. _____

_____

10. _____

_____

TEST IV

VI.   Write the books of the Old Testament in order. (39 points)

Use the word bank for correct spelling.

1. _____   21. _____
2. _____   22. _____
3. _____   23. _____
4. _____   24. _____
5. _____   25. _____
6. _____   26. _____
7. _____   27. _____
8. _____   28. _____
9. _____   29. _____
10. _____   30. _____
11. _____   31. _____
12. _____   32. _____
13. _____   33. _____
14. _____   34. _____
15. _____   35. _____
16. _____   36. _____
17. _____   37. _____
18. _____   38. _____
19. _____   39. _____
20. _____

I Kings	Leviticus	Malachi	Nahum
Amos	Judges	Nehemiah	Jeremiah
Isaiah	II Chronicles	Joel	Haggai
II Samuel	Numbers	Obadiah	Jonah
Ruth	Song of Solomon	Zechariah	Habakkuk
II Kings	Proverbs	Genesis	I Chronicles
Joshua	Ecclesiastes	Zephaniah	Exodus
Esther	Job	Hosea	I Samuel
Deuteronomy	Lamentations	Ezekiel	Psalms
Ezra	Daniel	Micah	

TEST IV

VII. Map. Write the correct number next to its location on the map below. (10 points)

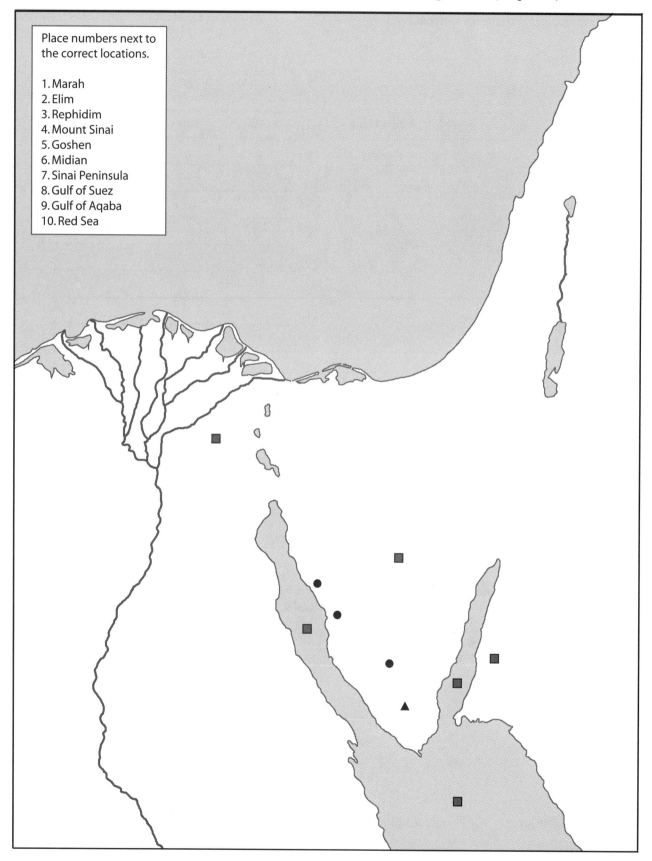

Place numbers next to
the correct locations.

1. Marah
2. Elim
3. Rephidim
4. Mount Sinai
5. Goshen
6. Midian
7. Sinai Peninsula
8. Gulf of Suez
9. Gulf of Aqaba
10. Red Sea

TEST V (87 total points) _____ Name

I.   Complete this memory verse: Deuteronomy 30:19 (5 points)

      I have set before you _____

      _____

II.   Matching. (8 points)

      _____ 1. King of Moabites   a. Eleazar

      _____ 2. Father of Moabites   b. brass serpent on pole

      _____ 3. Aaron's son   c. Lot

      _____ 4. People defeated by Israel before entering Canaan   d. Edomites

      _____ 5. Gave a blessing instead of a curse   e. Amorites

      _____ 6. King defeated by Israel before entering Canaan   f. Balaam

      _____ 7. Would cure the Israelites if they looked on it   g. Og, King of Bashan

      _____ 8. Refused to give passage to the Israelites   h. Balak

III. Vocabulary. Choose the correct word from the word bank. (7 points)

      ┌───┐
      │ countenance   murmur   scepter   │
      │ engrave   proclamation   stiff-necked   │
      │ frontlet   │
      └───┘

      1. to complain_____ 2. public announcement _____

      3. to carve designs into material_____ 4. case for scriptures_____

      5. symbol of power_____ 6. face _____

      7. stubborn _____

IV.   Identification. (8 points)

      1. Major river in the Holy Land _____

      2. A name for the Promised Land_____

      3. Said, "There are giants in the land!" _____

      4. Died on Mt. Nebo without entering the Promised Land _____

      5. What God said leads to life, and what leads to death_____

      6. Idol made by the Israelites at Mt. Sinai _____

      7. Length of time Israelites wandered in the wilderness _____

      8. Age of Moses when he died _____

V. Answer in complete sentences. (6 points)

1. Who led the people in the wrongdoing of making an idol? _____

_____

2. What did Moses do with the golden calf? _____

_____

3. Where did Moses put the stone tablets? _____

_____

VI. Number the events of Salvation History in order. (8 points)

_____ Noah's ark   _____ Call of Abraham

_____ Exodus   _____ Tower of Babel

_____ Fall of Man   _____ Creation

_____ Wilderness Wanderings   _____ The Sacrifice of Isaac

VII. Map. Write the correct number next to its location on each map. (6 points)

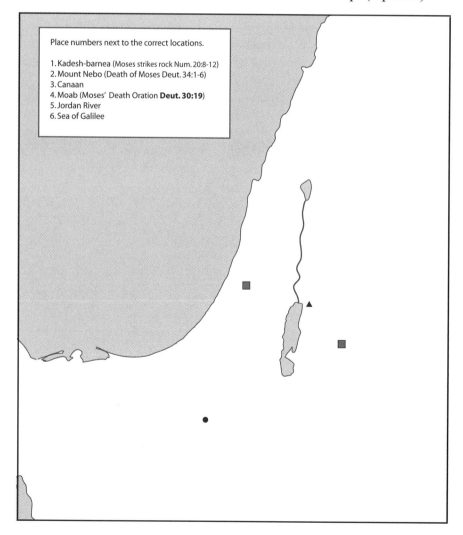

Place numbers next to the correct locations.

1. Kadesh-barnea (Moses strikes rock Num. 20:8-12)
2. Mount Nebo (Death of Moses Deut. 34:1-6)
3. Canaan
4. Moab (Moses' Death Oration **Deut. 30:19**)
5. Jordan River
6. Sea of Galilee

VIII. Write the books of the Old Testament in order. (39 points)

Use the word bank for correct spelling.

1. _____
2. _____
3. _____
4. _____
5. _____
6. _____
7. _____
8. _____
9. _____
10. _____
11. _____
12. _____
13. _____
14. _____
15. _____
16. _____
17. _____
18. _____
19. _____
20. _____

21. _____
22. _____
23. _____
24. _____
25. _____
26. _____
27. _____
28. _____
29. _____
30. _____
31. _____
32. _____
33. _____
34. _____
35. _____
36. _____
37. _____
38. _____
39. _____

I Kings	Leviticus	Malachi	Nahum
Amos	Judges	Nehemiah	Jeremiah
Isaiah	II Chronicles	Joel	Haggai
II Samuel	Numbers	Obadiah	Jonah
Ruth	Song of Solomon	Zechariah	Habakkuk
II Kings	Proverbs	Genesis	I Chronicles
Joshua	Ecclesiastes	Zephaniah	Exodus
Esther	Job	Hosea	I Samuel
Deuteronomy	Lamentations	Ezekiel	Psalms
Ezra	Daniel	Micah	

Christian Studies Final Test *(103 total points)*

Name: _____   Date: _____

Match the word or phrase to its definition. *(20 points)*

_____ 1. place where God placed man to enjoy life

_____ 2. the sin of Adam and Eve

_____ 3. father of many nations

_____ 4. "he who laughs"

_____ 5. the man who built the ark

_____ 6. Abraham's nephew

_____ 7. Abraham's wife

_____ 8. number of days and nights of the flood

_____ 9. wife of Isaac

_____ 10. most cunning of the beasts

_____ 11. symbol of God's covenant with man

_____ 12. tree that God forbid from Adam and Eve

_____ 13. act of God making everything that exists

_____ 14. where God confused language

_____ 15. angels of God

_____ 16. age of Abraham when Isaac was born

_____ 17. age of Sarah when Isaac was born

_____ 18. Adam and Eve's first sons

_____ 19. bird that Noah sent out to find dry land

_____ 20. Adam and Eve's third son

A. Abraham
B. Creation
C. Tower of Babel
D. Tree of Knowledge of Good and Evil
E. 100
F. rainbow
G. 40
H. Lot
I. Rebekah
J. Seth
K. Noah
L. The Fall of Man
M. Sarah
N. cherubim
O. 90
P. Garden of Eden
Q. Isaac
R. serpent
S. Cain and Abel
T. dove

Number the Biblical events in order. *(10 points)*

_____ Fall of Man

_____ Famine in Egypt

_____ Flood

_____ Twins Born to Struggle

_____ Joseph in Prison

_____ Passover

_____ Creation

_____ Tower of Babel

_____ Parting of the Red Sea

_____ Call of Abraham

Important Dates. *(2 points)*

1. Date of the Call of Abraham _____ B.C.

2. Date of Exodus _____ B.C.

Match the name or word to its definition. *(10 points)*

_____ 1. a crisis caused by lack of food

_____ 2. Jacob's beautiful wife

_____ 3. Isaac's oldest son

_____ 4. king of Egypt

_____ 5. Jacob's plain wife

_____ 6. favorite son of Jacob

_____ 7. Joseph's youngest brother

_____ 8. Isaac's son; received blessing

_____ 9. saved Joseph from death

_____ 10. Jacob's new name

A. Rachel
B. Leah
C. Jacob
D. famine
E. Reuben
F. Israel
G. Pharaoh
H. Joseph
I. Benjamin
J. Esau

List the Ten Commandments in order. *(10 points)*

1. The plague of _____

2. The plague of _____

3. The plague of _____

4. The plague of _____

5. The plague of _____

6. The plague of _____

7. The plague of _____

8. The plague of _____

9. The plague of _____

10. The plague of _____

List the Ten Commandments in order: *(10 points)*

1. Thou shalt _____

2. Thou shalt not _____

3. Thou shalt not _____

4. Remember _____

5. Honor _____

6. Thou shalt not _____

7. Thou shalt not _____

8. Thou shalt not _____

9. Thou shalt not _____

10. Thou shalt not _____

Match the name or word to its definition. *(10 points)*

_____ 1. held the Ten Commandments

_____ 2. day of rest

_____ 3. throne of pure gold

_____ 4. bread without yeast

_____ 5. tent with an altar

_____ 6. number of days Moses was in the mountains

_____ 7. brother of Moses

_____ 8. idol god the Hebrews made

_____ 9. bread provided by God

_____ 10. feast celebrating the Exodus of the Jews

A. golden calf
B. Passover
C. Sabbath
D. manna
E. unleavened bread
F. Ark of the Covenant
G. mercy seat
H. tabernacle
I. 40
J. Aaron

Answer the following questions with a phrase or sentence. *(7 points)*

1. What was the only command God gave Adam in the Garden of Eden?

_____

2. Who and what was to be let onto the ark?

_____

3. Write one of the three promises God made to Abraham.

_____

4. Who are the three patriarchs?

_____

5. What does the Hebrew word "Yahweh" mean?

6. How did the Israelites mark their homes so they were not victims of the last plague?

    _____

7. What was unique about Moses as a prophet?

    _____

Fill in the missing books of the Old Testament.
(24 points: 2 points each - 1 for the book's name, 1 for correct spelling)

Books of the Law:

1. Genesis

2. _____

3. Leviticus

4. Numbers

5. _____

Books of History:

1. Joshua

2. Judges

3. _____

4. I Samuel

5. II Samuel

6. _____

7. II Kings

8. I Chronicles

9. II Chronicles

10. Ezra

11. Nehemiah

12. _____

Books of Wisdom:

1. _____

2. Psalms

3. _____

4. Ecclesiastes

5. Song of Solomon

Major Prophets:

1. Isaiah

2. _____

3. Lamentations

4. Ezekiel

5. Daniel

Minor Prophets:

1. Hosea

2. Joel

3. _____

4. Obadiah

5. Jonah

6. Micah

7. _____

8. Habakkuk

9. Zephaniah

10. _____

11. Zechariah

12. _____

I.   Complete this memory verse: Genesis 12:1-3 (10 points)

Now the Lord said unto Abram, " _____

Get thee out of thy country and from thy kindred and from thy Father's house, unto a land that

I will shew thee; And I will make of thee a great nation and I will bless thee, and in thee all the

families of the Earth shall be blessed."

II.   Matching. (10 points)

_____f_____ 1. Adam and Eve's third son   a. Shem, Ham, Japheth

_____g_____ 2. Land between the rivers   b. Garden of Eden

_____d_____ 3. Sarah's handmaid, the mother of Ishmael   c. Sodom and Gomorrah

_____c_____ 4. Two wicked cities, destroyed by fire and brimstone d. Hagar

_____b_____ 5. Where God placed man to enjoy life   e. Ishmael

_____i_____ 6. He who laughs   f. Seth

_____h_____ 7. Mountain where Ark came to rest   g. Mesopotamia

_____j_____ 8. Modern Mesopotamia   h. Ararat

_____a_____ 9. Noah's sons   i. Isaac

_____e_____ 10. Son of Abraham and Hagar   j. Iraq

III.   Vocabulary. Choose the correct word from the word bank. (10 points)

cherubim	cunning	ex nihilo
cleave	dominion	imago Dei
covenant imago Dei	enmity	kindred
		sacred

1. image of God _____imago Dei_____   6. clever; crafty_____cunning_____

2. power; rule _____dominion_____   7. to join or unite with _____cleave_____

3. order of angels _____cherubim_____   8. out of nothing_____ex nihilo_____

4. relatives; tribe_____kindred_____   9. snake_____serpent_____

5. God's promise _____covenant_____   10. ill will _____enmity_____

IV.   Identification. (10 points)

1. Abraham's nephew_____Lot_____

2. Abraham's wife _____Sarah_____

3. Land given to Abraham as an inheritance _____Canaan_____

TEST I

4. Where God confused language ___Tower of Babel___

5. Date of Call of Abraham ___2000 B.C.___

6. Symbol of God's covenant with man ___rainbow___

7. She turned to a pillar of salt ___Lot's wife___

8. Adam and Eve's first two sons ___Cain and Abel___

9. Father of many nations ___Abraham___

10. Sin of Adam and Eve ___Fall of Man___

V.   Answer in complete sentences. (3 points each: 9 points)

1. How did God make woman? _____
   God put man into a deep sleep and then took one of man's ribs and made Woman.

2. What work did Cain do? What work did Abel do? __Cain grew food, tilled the ground.__
   Abel was a shepherd, a keeper of sheep.

3. How long did it rain? How long was the Great Flood upon the earth?_____
   It rained for 40 days and 40 nights. The flood was on the earth for 150 days.

VI.   Number the events of Salvation History in order. (6 points)

   __3__ First Murder

   __1__ The Creation

   __4__ The Flood

   __6__ Call of Abraham

   __2__ Fall of Man

   __5__ Tower of Babel

VII.   Number the days of Creation. (7 points)

   __6__ animals and humans   __3__ dry land, seas, plants

   __4__ sun, moon, stars   __7__ Sabbath, day of rest

   __5__ animals of seas and air   __1__ matter, light and dark, day and night

   __2__ sky; separated the waters

VIII.   Map. Write the correct number next to its location on each map that follows. (23 points)

Place numbers next to the correct locations.

1. Mesopotamia
2. Egypt
3. Africa
4. Arabia
5. Canaan
6. Ur
7. Haran
8. Mediterranean Sea
9. Red Sea
10. Tigris River
11. Euphrates River
12. Persian Gulf
13. Mt. Ararat

ASIA MINOR

Black Sea

Caspian Sea

3

8

2

9

5

11

7

13

4

10

1

6

12

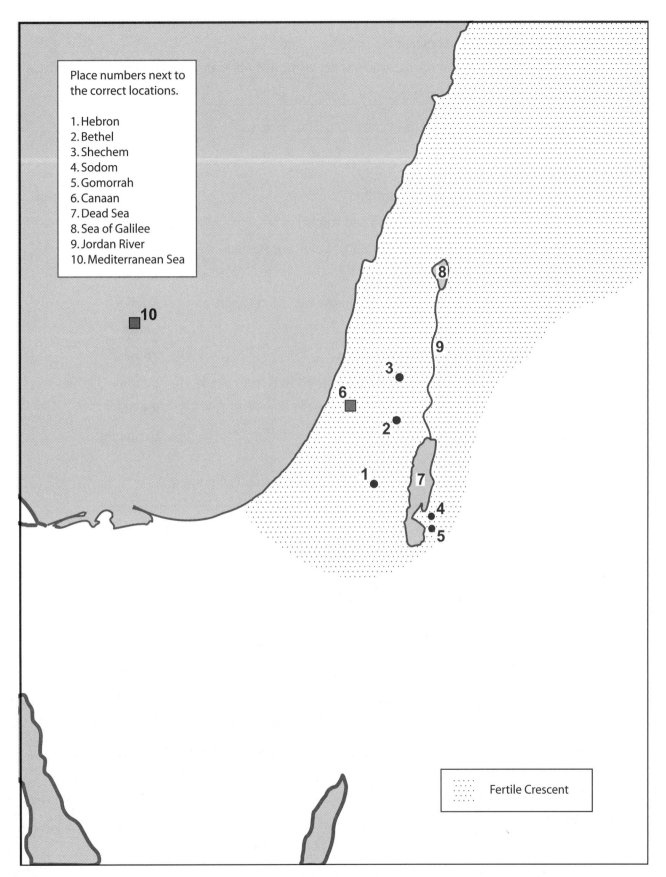

Place numbers next to
the correct locations.

1. Hebron
2. Bethel
3. Shechem
4. Sodom
5. Gomorrah
6. Canaan
7. Dead Sea
8. Sea of Galilee
9. Jordan River
10. Mediterranean Sea

Fertile Crescent

TEST II KEY (84 total points) _____ Name

I.   Complete this memory verse: Genesis 22:7-8 (10 points)

     And Isaac spake unto Abraham his father and said, " _____

     Behold the fire and the wood: but where is the lamb? And Abraham said, My son, God will provide

     himself a lamb for a burnt offering."

     _____

II.   Matching. (10 points)

     ___j___ 1. Joseph's youngest brother   a. Ephraim, Manasseh

     ___d___ 2. The two sons of Jacob and Rachel   b. Simeon

     ___f___ 3. Rebekah's brother; father of Leah and Rachel c. Leah

     ___c___ 4. Jacob's plain wife   d. Joseph, Benjamin

     ___b___ 5. Joseph's brother who was kept behind in Egypt e. Reuben

     ___h___ 6. She lied about Joseph   f. Laban

     ___i___ 7. Jacob's beautiful wife   g. Potiphar

     ___e___ 8. Joseph's oldest brother who saved him from death h. Potiphar's wife

     ___g___ 9. Egyptian who bought Joseph   i. Rachel

     ___a___ 10. Joseph's two sons   j. Benjamin

III. Vocabulary. Choose the correct word from the word bank. (10 points)

burnt offering	kine	score
butler	sackcloth	sheaf
famine	savory	venison
firstborn		

1. male servant _____butler_____   6. salty; flavorful _____savory_____

2. bundle of wheat _____sheaf_____   7. twenty _____score_____

3. cattle _____kine_____   8. deer meat _____venison_____

4. heir of blessing _____firstborn_____   9. mourning garment _____sackcloth_____

5. sacrifice to God_____burnt offering_____   10. complete lack of food_____famine_____

IV.   Identification. (10 points)

     1. Jacob's favorite son _____Joseph_____

     2. The three patriarchs _____Abraham, Isaac, Jacob_____

     3. Sold birthright for a mess of pottage _____Esau_____

     4. The king of Egypt_____Pharoah_____

140

5. Isaac's twin sons _____ Jacob and Esau

6. The three patriarch wives _____ Sarah, Rebekah, Rachel

7. Jacob's name was changed to _____ Israel

8. He had a coat of many colors _____ Joseph

9. Pharaoh's servants, in prison with Joseph _____ butler and baker

10. Number of years of plenty and famine _____ seven

V. Match the dreamer to the dream. (7 points)

   c   1. seven full ears and seven blasted ears   a. Joseph (2)

   a   2. your sheaves bowed down to my sheaf   b. baker

   e   3. ladder reaching to Heaven   c. Pharaoh (2)

   d   4. pressed grapes into Pharaoh's cup   d. butler

   c   5. seven fat cows and seven thin cows   e. Jacob

   b   6. birds ate from baskets of bread

   a   7. sun, moon, and stars bowed down to me

VI. Answer in complete sentences. (9 points)

1. Why did Esau sell his birthright? _____ Esau sold his future inheritance for something to eat immediately. He lived for the present rather than planning for the future.

2. Why did Joseph's brothers plot against him? Joseph's brothers were envious because Joseph was his father's favorite and because they feared that Joseph's dreams of ruling over them would come true.

3. What did the brothers find in their grain sacks on the way home? _____ The brothers found the money, with which they had paid for the grain.

TEST II

VII. Write the first 17 books of the Bible in order. (17 points)

Use the word bank for correct spelling.

1.	Genesis	10.	II Samuel
2.	Exodus	11.	I Kings
3.	Leviticus	12.	II Kings
4.	Numbers	13.	I Chronicles
5.	Deuteronomy	14.	II Chronicles
6.	Joshua	15.	Ezra
7.	Judges	16.	Nehemiah
8.	Ruth	17.	Esther
9.	I Samuel		

I Samuel	I Chronicles	II Kings	Ezra	Numbers
Genesis	Nehemiah	Joshua	Leviticus	
I Kings	II Samuel	Esther	Judges	
Exodus	Ruth	Deuteronomy	II Chronicles	

VIII. Map. Write the correct number next to its location on the map. (11 points)

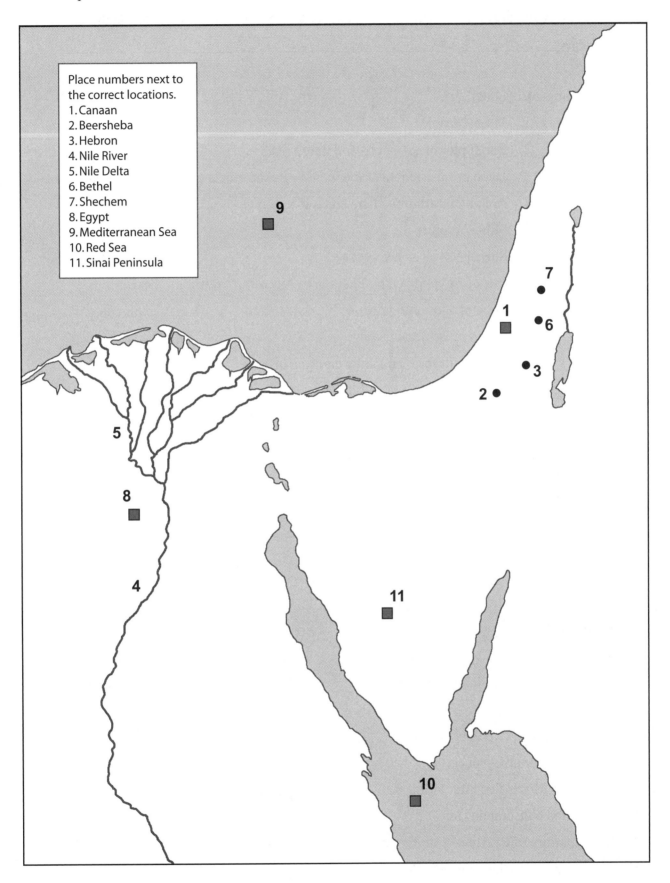

Place numbers next to the correct locations.
1. Canaan
2. Beersheba
3. Hebron
4. Nile River
5. Nile Delta
6. Bethel
7. Shechem
8. Egypt
9. Mediterranean Sea
10. Red Sea
11. Sinai Peninsula

TEST III (86 total points) _____ Name

I. Complete this memory verse: Exodus 7:3 (5 points)

And I will harden ____Pharaoh's heart, and multiply my signs and my wonders in the land of

Egypt._____

II. Matching. (10 points)

___d___ 1. Moses' sister
___f___ 2. Burial plot of patriarchs and their wives
___b___ 3. Jacob prophesied this tribe would rule the others
___j___ 4. Arc of land from the Persian Gulf to Egypt
___i___ 5. Moses' brother
___a___ 6. Raised Moses as her own son
___e___ 7. Part of Egypt given by Pharaoh to Joseph's family
___g___ 8. Tribe of Moses and Aaron
___h___ 9. Found in Benjamin's sack
___c___ 10. Cities built for Pharaoh by children of Israel

a. Pharaoh's daughter
b. Judah
c. Pithom and Ramses
d. Miriam
e. Goshen
f. Field of Machpelah
g. Levi
h. silver cup
i. Aaron
j. Fertile Crescent

III. Vocabulary. Choose the correct word from the word bank. (10 points)

caravan	Eve	plague
embalm	Judah	Yahweh
enchantment	midwife	yearn
	Moses	

1. "I will praise" ____Judah____
2. a destructive outbreak ____plague____
3. to wish for ____yearn____
4. "I am" ____Yahweh____
5. a train of pack animals ____caravan____
6. to preserve a dead body ____embalm____
7. mother of all living ____Eve____
8. magic spell ____enchantment____
9. "drawn out" ____Moses____
10. delivers babies ____midwife____

IV. Identification. (10 points)

1. Great river of Egypt ____Nile____
2. Where Moses fled after killing an Egyptian ____Midian____
3. Sea the Nile empties into ____Mediterranean____
4. Departure of Israelites from Egypt ____Exodus____
5. Direction in which the Nile flows ____north____

144

TEST III

6. Hidden in a basket on the Nile _____Moses_____

7. Meaning of "Yahweh" _____I am_____

8. How angel appeared to Moses on Mt. Horeb _____burning bush_____

9-10. Two names for God's people _____Israel; Hebrews_____

V. Answer in complete sentences. (9 points)

1. What did Pharaoh order midwives to do to Hebrew sons? _Pharaoh ordered the midwives attending Hebrew mothers to kill all male children._

2. Why did Moses flee from Egypt to the land of Midian? _Pharaoh was angry with Moses for killing one of his overseers who had struck one of the Hebrew workers._

3. What message did God send to Pharaoh through Moses and Aaron? _"Let my people go that they may worship me in the wilderness."_

VI. Number the events of Salvation History in order. (6 points)

_3_ Exile in Midian   _6_ Ten Plagues

_4_ Burning Bush   _5_ A Hard Heart

_1_ Baby Afloat on the Nile   _2_ The Murderer Flees

145

VII. Write the first 22 books of the Bible in order. (22 points)

Use the word bank for correct spelling.

1.	Genesis	12.	II Kings
2.	Exodus	13.	I Chronicles
3.	Leviticus	14.	II Chronicles
4.	Numbers	15.	Ezra
5.	Deuteronomy	16.	Nehemiah
6.	Joshua	17.	Esther
7.	Judges	18.	Job
8.	Ruth	19.	Psalms
9.	I Samuel	20.	Proverbs
10.	II Samuel	21.	Ecclesiastes
11.	I Kings	22.	Song of Solomon

I Samuel	II Samuel	Ezra	Song of Solomon
Genesis	Ruth	Leviticus	Proverbs
I Kings	II Kings	Judges	Ecclesiastes
Exodus	Joshua	II Chronicles	Job
I Chronicles	Esther	Numbers	
Nehemiah	Deuteronomy	Psalms	

VIII. Map. Write the correct number next to its location on the map. (14 points)

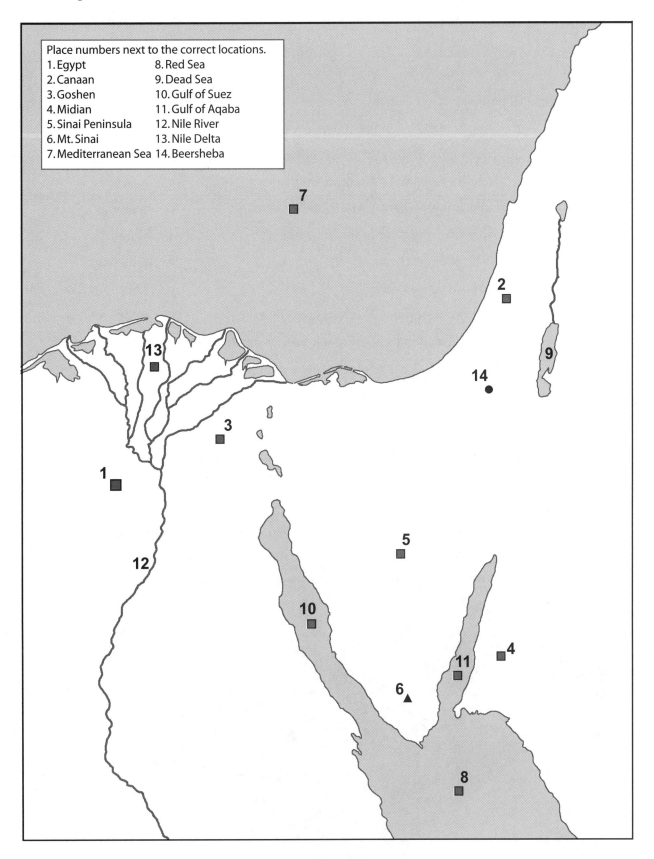

Place numbers next to the correct locations.
1. Egypt   8. Red Sea
2. Canaan   9. Dead Sea
3. Goshen   10. Gulf of Suez
4. Midian   11. Gulf of Aqaba
5. Sinai Peninsula 12. Nile River
6. Mt. Sinai   13. Nile Delta
7. Mediterranean Sea 14. Beersheba

_____ Name

I.   Complete this memory verse: Exodus 31:18 (5 points)

And he gave unto Moses <u>upon Mount Sinai two tablets of stone, written with the finger of God.</u>

_____

II.   Matching. (10 points)

_h_ 1. Figures at either end of the mercy seat	a. showbread
_j_ 2. To strongly desire that which belongs to another	b. mercy seat
_g_ 3. Held the Law and the Commandments	c. Jethro
_b_ 4. Golden throne on the Ark of the Covenant	d. menorah
_d_ 5. 7-branch lampstand in the Tabernacle	e. Marah
_i_ 6. To lie about someone	f. Amalekites
_c_ 7. Moses' father-in-law	g. Ark of the Covenant
_e_ 8. Bitter waters in the Wilderness of Shur	h. golden angels
_a_ 9. Bread placed in the Tabernacle each Sabbath	i. bear false witness
_f_ 10. Defeated by the Israelites on the way to Mt. Sinai	j. covet

III.   Number the items of the Tabernacle corresponding to names in the word bank. (8 points)

1. Altar of Incense	2. Lampstand
3. Most Holy Place	4. Laver
5. Ark of the Covenant	6. Altar of Burnt Offering
7. Table of Showbread	8. Holy Place

5. Ark of Covenant

3. Most Holy Place

1. Altar of Incense

7. Table of Showbread

8. Holy Place

2. Lampstand

4. Laver

6. Altar of Burnt Offering

TEST IV

IV. Identification. (10 points)

1. Bread that rained from Heaven in the desert _____ manna
2. He spoke directly with God _____ Moses
3. Feast celebrating the Exodus from Egypt _____ Passover
4. Number of days Moses was on Mt. Sinai _____ 40
5. What the children of Israel always did when difficulties arose _____ murmur
6. Mountain where God gave the Law and the Commandments _____ Mt. Sinai
7. Great miracle of the Exodus _____ parting of the Red Sea
8. Defeated the Amalekites when Moses raised his hands _____ Joshua
9. Tribe the priests of Israel came from _____ Levi
10. Tent that served as a portable sanctuary _____ Tabernacle

V. Write the Ten Commandments. (10 points)

1. Thou shalt have no other gods before Me.

2. Thou shalt not make unto thee any graven image.

3. Thou shalt not take the name of the Lord thy God in vain.

4. Remember the Sabbath day, to keep it holy.

5. Honor thy father and thy mother.

6. Thou shalt not kill.

7. Thou shalt not commit adultery.

8. Thou shalt not steal.

9. Thou shalt not bear false witness.

10. Thou shalt not covet thy neighbor's wife, nor anything that is thy neighbor's.

TEST IV

VI. Write the books of the Old Testament in order. (39 points)

Use the word bank for correct spelling.

1.	Genesis	21.	Ecclesiastes
2.	Exodus	22.	Song of Solomon
3.	Leviticus	23.	Isaiah
4.	Numbers	24.	Jeremiah
5.	Deuteronomy	25.	Lamentations
6.	Joshua	26.	Ezekiel
7.	Judges	27.	Daniel
8.	Ruth	28.	Hosea
9.	I Samuel	29.	Joel
10.	II Samuel	30.	Amos
11.	I Kings	31.	Obadiah
12.	II Kings	32.	Jonah
13.	I Chronicles	33.	Micah
14.	II Chronicles	34.	Nahum
15.	Ezra	35.	Habakkuk
16.	Nehemiah	36.	Zephaniah
17.	Esther	37.	Haggai
18.	Job	38.	Zechariah
19.	Psalms	39.	Malachi
20.	Proverbs		

I Kings	Leviticus	Malachi	Nahum
Amos	Judges	Nehemiah	Jeremiah
Isaiah	II Chronicles	Joel	Haggai
II Samuel	Numbers	Obadiah	Jonah
Ruth	Song of Solomon	Zechariah	Habakkuk
II Kings	Proverbs	Genesis	I Chronicles
Joshua	Ecclesiastes	Zephaniah	Exodus
Esther	Job	Hosea	I Samuel
Deuteronomy	Lamentations	Ezekiel	Psalms
Ezra	Daniel	Micah	

150

TEST IV

VII. Map. Write the correct number next to its location on the map. (10 points)

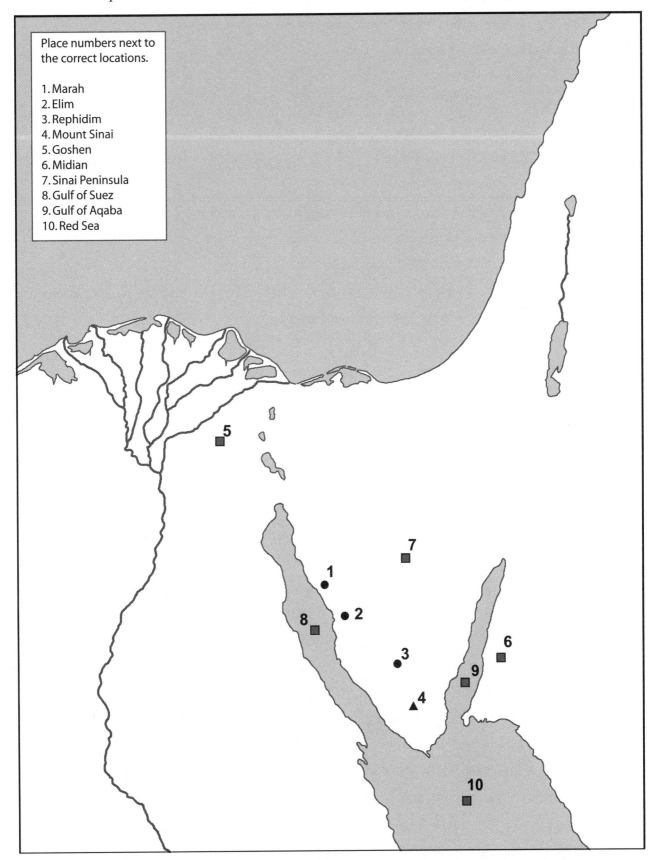

Place numbers next to
the correct locations.

1. Marah
2. Elim
3. Rephidim
4. Mount Sinai
5. Goshen
6. Midian
7. Sinai Peninsula
8. Gulf of Suez
9. Gulf of Aqaba
10. Red Sea

_____ Name

I. Complete this memory verse: Deuteronomy 30:19 (5 points)

I have set before you ___life and death, blessing and cursing; therefore choose life, that both

thou and thy seed may live.___

II. Matching. (8 points)

_h_	1. King of Moabites		a.	Eleazar
_c_	2. Father of Moabites		b.	brass serpent on pole
_a_	3. Aaron's son		c.	Lot
_e_	4. People defeated by Israel before entering Canaan		d.	Edomites
_f_	5. Gave a blessing instead of a curse		e.	Amorites
_g_	6. King defeated by Israel before entering Canaan		f.	Balaam
_b_	7. Would cure the Israelites if they looked on it		g.	Og, King of Bashan
_d_	8. Refused to give passage to the Israelites		h.	Balak

III. Vocabulary. Choose the correct word from the word bank. (7 points)

countenance	murmur	scepter
engrave	proclamation	stiff-necked
frontlet		

1. complain _____murmur_____   2. public announcement ___proclamation___
3. to carve designs into material _engrave_   4. small case for scriptures _frontlet_
5. symbol of power _____scepter_____   6. face _____countenance____
7. stubborn _____stiff-necked_____

IV. Identification. (8 points)

1. Major river in the Holy Land _____Jordan River_____
2. A name for the Promised Land_____land of milk and honey____
3. Said, "There are giants in the land!" _____the faithless spies_____
4. Died on Mt. Nebo without entering the Promised Land ___Moses_____
5. What God said leads to life, and what leads to death____obedience; disobedience__
6. Idol made by the Israelites at Mt. Sinai _____golden calf_____
7. Length of time Israelites wandered in the wilderness ____40 years_____
8. Age of Moses when he died _____120_____

V. Answer in complete sentences. (6 points)

1. Who led the people in the wrongdoing of making an idol? _____

Aaron led the people in this wrongdoing. _____

2. What did Moses do with the golden calf? __Moses burned the golden calf and ground the__

melted gold into a powder that he sprinkled on the people's drinking water. _____

3. Where did Moses put the stone tablets? __Moses placed the tablets in the Ark of the__

Covenant in the Tabernacle. _____

VI. Number the events of Salvation History in order. (8 points)

_3_	Noah's ark	_5_	Call of Abraham
_7_	Exodus	_4_	Tower of Babel
_2_	Fall of Man	_1_	Creation
_8_	Wilderness Wanderings	_6_	The Sacrifice of Isaac

VII. Map. Write the correct number next to its location on each map. (6 points)

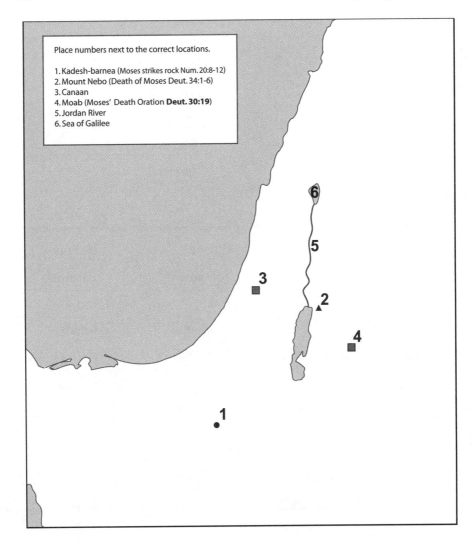

Place numbers next to the correct locations.

1. Kadesh-barnea (Moses strikes rock Num. 20:8-12)
2. Mount Nebo (Death of Moses Deut. 34:1-6)
3. Canaan
4. Moab (Moses' Death Oration **Deut. 30:19**)
5. Jordan River
6. Sea of Galilee

TEST V

VIII. Write the books of the Old Testament in order. (39 points)

Use the word bank for correct spelling.

1. _____ Genesis
2. _____ Exodus
3. _____ Leviticus
4. _____ Numbers
5. _____ Deuteronomy
6. _____ Joshua
7. _____ Judges
8. _____ Ruth
9. _____ I Samuel
10. _____ II Samuel
11. _____ I Kings
12. _____ II Kings
13. _____ I Chronicles
14. _____ II Chronicles
15. _____ Ezra
16. _____ Nehemiah
17. _____ Esther
18. _____ Job
19. _____ Psalms
20. _____ Proverbs

21. _____ Ecclesiastes
22. _____ Song of Solomon
23. _____ Isaiah
24. _____ Jeremiah
25. _____ Lamentations
26. _____ Ezekiel
27. _____ Daniel
28. _____ Hosea
29. _____ Joel
30. _____ Amos
31. _____ Obadiah
32. _____ Jonah
33. _____ Micah
34. _____ Nahum
35. _____ Habakkuk
36. _____ Zephaniah
37. _____ Haggai
38. _____ Zechariah
39. _____ Malachi

I Kings	Leviticus	Malachi	Nahum
Amos	Judges	Nehemiah	Jeremiah
Isaiah	II Chronicles	Joel	Haggai
II Samuel	Numbers	Obadiah	Jonah
Ruth	Song of Solomon	Zechariah	Habakkuk
II Kings	Proverbs	Genesis	I Chronicles
Joshua	Ecclesiastes	Zephaniah	Exodus
Esther	Job	Hosea	I Samuel
Deuteronomy	Lamentations	Ezekiel	Psalms
Ezra	Daniel	Micah	

Christian Studies Final Test KEY *(103 total points)*

Name: _____ Date: _____

Match the word or phrase to its definition. *(20 points)*

___P___ 1. place where God placed man to enjoy life

___L___ 2. the sin of Adam and Eve

___A___ 3. father of many nations

___Q___ 4. "he who laughs"

___K___ 5. the man who built the ark

___H___ 6. Abraham's nephew

___M___ 7. Abraham's wife

___G___ 8. number of days and nights of the flood

___I___ 9. wife of Isaac

___R___ 10. most cunning of the beasts

___F___ 11. symbol of God's covenant with man

___D___ 12. tree that God forbid from Adam and Eve

___B___ 13. act of God making everything that exists

___C___ 14. where God confused language

___N___ 15. angels of God

___E___ 16. age of Abraham when Isaac was born

___O___ 17. age of Sarah when Isaac was born

___S___ 18. Adam and Eve's first sons

___T___ 19. bird that Noah sent out to find dry land

___J___ 20. Adam and Eve's third son

A. Abraham
B. Creation
C. Tower of Babel
D. Tree of Knowledge of Good and Evil
E. 100
F. rainbow
G. 40
H. Lot
I. Rebekah
J. Seth
K. Noah
L. The Fall of Man
M. Sarah
N. cherubim
O. 90
P. Garden of Eden
Q. Isaac
R. serpent
S. Cain and Abel
T. dove

Number the Biblical events in order. *(10 points)*

___2___ Fall of Man

___8___ Famine in Egypt

___3___ Flood

___6___ Twins Born to Struggle

___7___ Joseph in Prison

___9___ Passover

___1___ Creation

___4___ Tower of Babel

___10___ Parting of the Red Sea

___5___ Call of Abraham

155

Christian Studies Final Test

Important Dates. *(2 points)*

1. Date of the Call of Abraham _____ *2000* B.C.

2. Date of Exodus _____ *1400* B.C.

Match the name or word to its definition. *(10 points)*

_*D*_ 1. a crisis caused by lack of food

_*A*_ 2. Jacob's beautiful wife

_*J*_ 3. Isaac's oldest son

_*G*_ 4. king of Egypt

_*B*_ 5. Jacob's plain wife

_*H*_ 6. favorite son of Jacob

_*I*_ 7. Joseph's youngest brother

_*C*_ 8. Isaac's son; received blessing

_*E*_ 9. saved Joseph from death

_*F*_ 10. Jacob's new name

A. Rachel
B. Leah
C. Jacob
D. famine
E. Reuben
F. Israel
G. Pharaoh
H. Joseph
I. Benjamin
J. Esau

List the 10 plagues in order. *(10 points)*

1. The plague of _*water and blood*_

2. The plague of _*frogs*_

3. The plague of _*lice*_

4. The plague of _*flies*_

5. The plague of _*cattle*_

6. The plague of _*sores*_

7. The plague of _*hail and fire*_

8. The plague of _*locusts*_

9. The plague of _*darkness*_

10. The plague of _*death of the firstborn*_

List the Ten Commandments in order. *(10 points)*

1. Thou shalt _*have no other gods before Me*_

2. Thou shalt not _*make any graven image*_

156

Christian Studies Final Test

3. Thou shalt not _take the name of the Lord in vain_

4. Remember _the Sabbath, to keep it holy_

5. Honor _thy father and mother_

6. Thou shalt not _kill_

7. Thou shalt not _commit adultery_

8. Thou shalt not _steal_

9. Thou shalt not _bear false witness_

10. Thou shalt not _covet thy neighbor's wife or belongings_

Match each name or word to its definition. *(10 points)*

_F_ 1. held the Ten Commandments

_C_ 2. day of rest

_G_ 3. throne of pure gold

_E_ 4. bread without yeast

_H_ 5. tent with an altar

_I_ 6. number of days Moses was in the mountains

_J_ 7. brother of Moses

_A_ 8. idol god the Hebrews made

_D_ 9. bread provided by God

_B_ 10. feast celebrating the Exodus of the Jews

A. golden calf
B. Passover
C. Sabbath
D. manna
E. unleavened bread
F. Ark of the Covenant
G. mercy seat
H. tabernacle
I. 40
J. Aaron

Answer the following questions with a phrase or sentence. *(7 points)*

1. What was the only command God gave Adam in the Garden of Eden?

    Do not eat from the Tree of Knowledge of Good and Evil.

2. Who and what was to be let onto the ark?

    Noah, his wife, his sons and their wives, and two of each kind of animal

3. Write one of the three promises God made to Abraham.   _1. He would have a son through Sarah._

    2. His descendants would be as numerous as the stars. 3. He would inherit the land of Canaan.

4. Who are the three patriarchs?

    Abraham, Isaac, Jacob

5. What does the Hebrew word "Yahweh" mean?

    "I AM" or "He who is"

6. How did the Israelites mark their homes so they were not victims of the last plague?

   They marked the doorposts of their homes with the blood of a sacrificed lamb.

7. What was unique about Moses as a prophet?

   Moses spoke to the Lord face-to-face.

Fill in the missing books of the Old Testament.

(24 points: 2 points each - 1 for the book's name, 1 for correct spelling)

Books of the Law:

1. Genesis
2. *Exodus*
3. Leviticus
4. Numbers
5. *Deuteronomy*

Books of History:

1. Joshua
2. Judges
3. *Ruth*
4. I Samuel
5. II Samuel
6. *I Kings*
7. II Kings
8. I Chronicles
9. II Chronicles
10. Ezra
11. Nehemiah
12. *Esther*

Books of Wisdom:

1. *Job*
2. Psalms
3. *Proverbs*
4. Ecclesiastes
5. Song of Solomon

Major Prophets:

1. Isaiah
2. *Jeremiah*
3. Lamentations
4. Ezekiel
5. Daniel

Minor Prophets:

1. Hosea
2. Joel
3. *Amos*
4. Obadiah
5. Jonah
6. Micah
7. *Nahum*
8. Habakkuk
9. Zephaniah
10. *Haggai*
11. Zechariah
12. *Malachi*